Keys to Successful Interviewing

KEYS TO
SUCCESSFUL
INTERVIEWING

STEWART HARRAL

UNIVERSITY OF OKLAHOMA PRESS : NORMAN

By Stewart Harral

Keys to Successful Interviewing
(Norman, 1954)
Tested Public Relations for Schools
(Norman, 1952)
Patterns of Publicity Copy
(Norman, 1950)
Public Relations for Churches
(New York & Nashville, 1945)
Public Relations for Higher Education
(Norman, 1942)
Successful Letters for Churches
(New York & Nashville, 1946)
Publicity Problems (editor)
(Norman, 1940)

Library of Congress Catalog Card Number: 54–5929

Copyright 1954 by the University of Oklahoma Press
Publishing Division of the University
Composed and Printed at Norman, Oklahoma, U.S.A.
by the University of Oklahoma Press
First Edition

To H. H. Herbert
Teacher   Friend   Counselor
Whose Former Students Cover
the Newsfronts of the World

Contents

Why You Need This Book

THIS BOOK is a tool, a tool to help you get better answers to your questions. It is for many people engaged in a wide variety of occupations:

Reporters who must get the news—facts and opinions—from all types of persons;

Publicity and public relations workers who must get facts for their programs of interpretation;

Journalism students—high school, junior college, and university—who must learn the art of interviewing;

Radio and television newscasters who must evoke responses in varied interviewing situations;

Writers who must travel and interview scores of persons for background material for stories and features;

Public opinion pollers who rely on the interview as the most important tool in getting comments;

Magazine editors and staff members who must ask the right questions in the right way to get news and information;

Foreign correspondents who must "get the news and get it first" in complex situations;

Advertising copy writers and research investigators who must develop their skills as interviewers to learn all possible about their prospects, the consumers;

Photographers—still, motion picture, newsreel, and television—who must know effective interviewing techniques to get people to respond to their requests;

Information specialists who must obtain technical data from all types of respondents, ranging from the garrulous to the reticent;

Columnists who are eager to get "the news behind the headlines";

Fiction writers who must search out facts and color material for their stories.

Streamlined media—radio, television, newsreels, magazines, and newspapers—bring news, pictures, personalities, and events to Mr. Average Man as he sits in his living room. The gathering and transmission of news from all over the world is a modern miracle. But one fact remains unchanged: all interviewers, no matter what channel or media they represent, must still ask questions to get news and comments.

Do modern writers rely too much on the telephone? Do they lean too heavily on publicity handouts? Do their stories lack the color and sparkle which come only from face-to-face interviewing? Carl Lindstrom, managing editor of the *Hartford Times,* thinks so. Writing in *Nieman Reports,* he declares that it is impossible to separate good reporting from observation. And then he asks, "How do you observe the twinkle in the eye, the glint of anger, or the reflective glance of a defense mechanism going into gear? Can you get it over the telephone? Hardly."

Certain factors are common to all interviewing, whether by the psychiatrist or by the newsman. But the interview as employed by the writer usually has one of the following objectives: to explore another's mind or sentiments, to obtain information in regard to specific situations or attitudes, or to get a person to talk about something which will interest readers. It is this last objective which makes the journalistic interview wholly different from other types of interviews.

You can't list all the requirements for a successful interview as you list the ingredients of a cake, because each situation is unique and requires special knowledge on the part of the interviewer. He must, for example, have a knowledge of environmental forces, news values, human behavior, and interviewing skills and techniques—all focused on getting information, comments, and opinions from individuals. Because the interview is not confined to facts, it is more than the sum of its parts. It is in itself an entity.

Until now no one has considered it necessary to devote a book to the subject of strategies of interviewing for writers. A chapter or two in books or brief articles in professional journals have been deemed sufficient. If a successful interview boils down to the familiar platitudes of getting ready, asking the right questions, and knowing the interviewee, you may well ask, "Why say more?"

First of all, writers from time to time forget the fundamentals of effective interviewing and need a ready reference to refresh their memories, especially since interviews provide the basis for practically all stories. In addition, skillful writers, who have never before analyzed or disclosed their interviewing techniques, discuss their methods so that others may profit from them.

This book is based on four propositions: (1) Effective interviewing is an art; (2) at least 90 per cent of all material for all news stories (press, radio, magazine, and television) must be obtained by interviews; (3) successful interviewing comes from using a wide variety of psychological principles and techniques; and (4) research has discovered and isolated many of these approaches and principles, so that you can use certain tested techniques in stepping up your own interviewing skills.

It is my hope that this book will be a sort of road map for all who set out on adventures in interviewing. As

Korzybyski, in discussing semantics, says about words, this book is the map, not the territory; but it gives some idea of the region to be covered and the general direction to be taken. Perhaps it will keep the person already embarked on his journey off side roads and shorten and speed his travel.

In preparing this volume, I made an exhaustive study of the literature on the interview, not in journalism alone, but in law, medicine, education, psychiatry, the ministry, personnel work, marketing, social case work, and other areas. I sought suggestions from scores of successful reporters and writers—those who have won Pulitzer prizes, Nieman fellowships, Sigma Delta Chi awards, and other distinctions. Finally, I summarized techniques which have proved successful in my own experience and which I have observed being used effectively by fellow workers.

It is impossible to trace the origin of some of the material in this book, especially of suggestions for stepping up an interviewer's skills—each idea started with someone, and it has been passed along until its creator's identity has been lost. To many authors of books and magazine articles in allied fields I am sure I owe a debt, but one too diffused and nebulous to detail. A man will see his shadow here or there and say, "There am I."

When I first proposed this study, some newsmen urged that I "forget the idea." Many were skeptical of the outcome. Others questioned the advisability of attempting to set any standards of success.

Why such skepticism? A few newsmen felt that the interview is such an intangible thing, complicated by so many variables, that to control it or standardize it, or even analyze it, is impossible.

However, I was convinced that the process of interviewing could be studied with the hope of definite and practical results. It is true that many skilled interviewers found it difficult to describe the techniques they use or to indicate the factors contributing to their success. And yet I knew they had acquired certain techniques—valuable "know-how" —which they could share with others.

This book is not intended to be the final answer, the master plan, to all phases of interviewing. Nor can it transform any reporter into an expert interviewer. Rather, its chief aim is to help all writers—reporters, publicity writers, radio newsmen, free-lance writers, historians, news association staffers, and others—not through a neat little formula, but through the use of psychologically sound principles.

Furthermore, this volume deals with fundamental principles as well as practical and result-getting ideas. Many well-known writers reveal their "secrets" of interviewing. In fact, so far as I know, many of the subjects here discussed have never been treated previously in any publication.

This volume is meant as a guidebook and manual for both the veteran reporter and for the beginning student in journalism. In addition, it can be used as a textbook because it presents in organized form an overview of the wide scope and tremendous possibilities of interviewing.

Five years have been required to complete the research and writing for this book. In the process, I have incurred a heavy debt to many people for friendly encouragement, wise counsel, and information generously provided. I owe a real debt of gratitude to my colleague, Dwight V. Swain, for his helpful advice and encouragement. To Irene Elliott and Lou DeWees, I am indebted for typing assistance. Finally, I wish to acknowledge my obligation to scores of persons who supplied comments and illustrative material. It is not possible to mention them by name here, but their courtesy and helpful interest are not forgotten.

Stewart Harral

Norman, Oklahoma
January 20, 1954

Keys to Successful Interviewing

1

Know-how Makes the Difference

WHY wouldn't Herbert Hoover talk? About all he would say was "Yes" or "No" as Paul Leach, correspondent for the *Chicago Daily News*, kept trying to kindle his interest. He tried touching on Hoover's pet subjects—and nothing happened. Here he was on Hoover's special train, in Hoover's private car, with the undivided attention of the famous American. Here was a chance for a dramatic interview. But Leach was drawing a blank.

Then something happened. Leach made a misstatement of fact about something he knew very well. The train was crossing Nevada. Leach looked out the window at the dreary wasteland and said, "This is still the country of the pick-and-shovel prospector." Hoover answered immediately and for an hour told how modern mining methods had displaced the old aimless prospecting. Furthermore, he talked about petroleum, air mail, and other topics.

At that moment, Mr. Hoover was one of the most important men in the world. As Republican candidate for the presidency of the United States, he was on his way to Palo Alto for the ceremony to notify him formally of his nomination.

How did Leach spark Hoover into talking for nearly two hours? How did he get a feature interview? He succeeded by revealing his own ignorance and giving Hoover a chance to correct him. He touched Hoover's ego; he made him feel important.

Harold A. Littledale, an enterprising reporter for the *New York Evening Post,* suspected that something was wrong at the New Jersey State Prison at Trenton. So he started an extensive investigation. He quizzed many persons. The result was a tale of horror. He showed that the prison was monstrous, medieval, unhealthy, and overcrowded.

Littledale's dramatic report stirred up a hornets' nest in New Jersey. Immediately the governor appointed a commission to investigate the charges. Three weeks later he found a report on his desk listing a series of basic reforms. Littledale was awarded the 1918 Pulitzer Prize in reporting.

He demonstrated a trait which made him successful and famous. He used interviewing to blow the lid off a disgraceful situation. He kept asking questions.

"Newspaper writing," the late Henry Justin Smith once told a class in journalism, "is hard, and it grinds your brains to powder. You don't burn yourself up, though. You get hardened like steel. And your literary style becomes like steel, too." To the man who gets his greatest satisfaction out of writing, making the front page is the elixir of life.

One reporter who made the front page was Ben Hecht—newspaperman, author, playwright, and scenarist. His vitality and roaring gusto made him a legend in many newsrooms. He looked tough, and he was tough. How did he operate? Watch him in action.

Chicago—the scene of many violent deaths—was not too excited about the killing of the ragged stranger. A young World War I veteran, Carl Oscar Wanderer, had re-

4

turned home to Chicago, married his childhood sweetheart, and gone to work in his father's butcher shop. One night on the way home from a movie, the Wanderers were followed by a ragged young gunman who attempted a holdup. The war veteran shot it out with him. In the scuffle, his bride was fatally wounded. A policeman arriving at the scene found Wanderer firing bullets into the already dead body of the gunman. The coroner's jury brought in a verdict against John Doe, the unknown tramp, and expressed its condolences to Wanderer on the loss of his wife. It also congratulated him on his courage in killing the gunman.

Young Ben Hecht of the *Chicago Daily News* sniffed a story and went to interview the hero. He found Wanderer at home, seemingly unconcerned about the death of his wife. Hecht sensed that something was wrong. At his instigation police investigated and discovered the two guns found at the scene of the killing had both been in Wanderer's possession the day before the incident. Wanderer, apparently in deadly fear of a life of domesticity, had hired the tramp to stage the holdup. But Wanderer did not follow the script; instead, he had shot both his wife and the tramp with the same gun. He was found guilty of the murder of his wife and the ragged stranger and condemned to death.

> How did Hecht sense that something was wrong? He sized up the situation. He felt sure that Wanderer's actions and words were not consistent. Hecht was alert and skeptical; he "saw through" the situation.

Are you ready when the "big moment" comes?

Walter Duranty, foreign correspondent for the *New York Times,* was sitting in his room in Moscow one evening in the summer of 1924 when his telephone rang. The acting chief of the press department of the Foreign Office requested his presence at once.

5

"I am taking you to a trial," the acting chief informed Duranty when he met him. He explained that only two other correspondents would be admitted. "It is the trial of our greatest enemy. . . . tonight the Supreme Military Tribunal of the U.S.S.R. will pass judgment on its archenemy, Boris Savinkov, Kerensky's war minister, who planned the killing of Count Mirbach and the attempted assassination of Lenin. He came to Russia secretly, in disguise and with false papers, but we caught him; and tonight he will be judged."

Duranty came out of the trial with one of the greatest stories of his career. "I will always think of it as the greatest theatrical performance I ever attended," Duranty wrote later.

His secret: He was ready to move in on a big story at the right moment.

You won't always get your interview in an atmosphere of ease and luxury.

On a cold winter day in early 1925, young Floyd Collins was prowling underground in his native Kentucky in search of new cavern wonders to attract tourists. He found a marvelous, great new cavern, just a few miles from Mammoth Cave. Suddenly, when less than one hundred feet from daylight, he was caught in a cave-in that pinned his foot under a six-ton boulder. He was imprisoned, imprisoned in a natural tomb, with rocks, gravel, and mud covering him to the hips.

William Burke ("Skeets") Miller, reporter for the *Louisville Courier-Journal*, rushed to Sand Cave to cover the story. When he reached the spot, he found several friends of the man wondering how soon Collins would free himself. Miller promptly organized rescue squads. Several times he crawled on his stomach down into a black, slippery passage to interview the trapped man. Miller's stories won him the 1926 Pulitzer Prize in reporting.

6

How did Miller accomplish this feat? He saw the
news possibilities in interviewing the trapped man.
He was cut by the rocks, his body was numbed by
the cold, he was exhausted. He risked danger to
bring news to millions of anxious readers.

For weeks, Ira Cain, military editor of the *Fort
Worth Star-Telegram,* had been working to get a beat. He
hoped to report the maiden flight at Fort Worth of Consoli-
dated Vultee's new YB-60, the jet version of the B-36 bomber.

Officials from the Pentagon arrived at the plant,
dropped a curtain of security over the flight date, and barred
all reporters. Cain wasn't stopped. Every day he drove his
car as close as he could get to the test field. One day he
noticed that something dropped from a flight of B-36's over-
head. It shot away so fast that it was obviously either a rocket
or jet fighter.

He quizzed sources: "What did I see?" He got only
blank stares. Finally, as the officials started back to Washington, one officer told Cain, "Don't write about it, and I'll see
if I can get it released."

Then came the telephone call giving Cain his scoop.
The story: Convair had turned a B-36 and an F-84 jet fighter
into a "mother-daughter" team. Wire services carried Cain's
story around the country.

Cain's secret: Although rebuffed, he did not get
off the story. He watched. He waited. Then when
he was sure, he quizzed his news source. Soon afterwards his belief was confirmed. He scooped the nation.

Now that you've seen a few experts in action, perhaps you are asking, "What makes a great reporter? What
traits are needed by 'big league' interviewers?"

First of all, no person is a born interviewer. Secondly, an analysis of the methods of hundreds of successful

reporters shows that no two of them are alike. Each writer blends a different combination of traits, characteristics, and methods. One top-flight reporter's dominant characteristic may be a sparkling enthusiasm. The man at the next desk may employ a great persuasiveness with success. Another has developed a skillful use of questions. Here is a city hall reporter whose sure knowledge of his run is the big secret of his front-page stories. There is the feature writer whose special aptitude for capturing turns of speech gives his stories spontaneity and color.

Dominant traits in reporters may differ, but all skilled interviewers possess specific and clearly defined techniques and characteristics in a greater or less degree. These patterns—these KEYS TO SUCCESSFUL INTERVIEWING—will be revealed to you in the pages that follow. One thing is certain. By adding any of these strategies to your present stock of "know-how," you will become a more effective interviewer. And when you use all of them, you are certain to step up your effectiveness in one of the most fascinating and difficult of all arts, the art of interviewing.

2

Are People Predictable?

In St. Joseph, Missouri, the Reverend Adiel J. Moncrief lost his gold pocket watch while visiting with his congregation after preaching a sermon entitled "What Time Is It?"

In Detroit, high school football player Alex Jones knocked himself out crashing head first into a steel post, later groggily explained, "I run faster with my eyes shut."

In Tulsa, motorist Walter Mims explained to police why he had hit a woman driver: "She signaled she was going to turn right, and then she turned right."

Louise Springer confessed that she went for treatment to six Chicago dentists and, while they bent over her with the drill, picked their pockets for a total take of $2,000.

In Rio de Janeiro, after a snake bit him, Francisco Feliciano chased and caught the viper and bit it to death.

Amusing? Unbelievable? Interesting? These items, published in the "Miscellany" column in *Time*, show some of the queer things which people do. Why did these people believe and act as they did? Are people predictable? How can you step up your interviewing techniques by tying them in with psychological drives and urges?

Only in Hollywood does the reporter give advice to foreign ministers. Only on celluloid and in some television shows do writers live in the rarefied atmosphere inhabited

9

by kings and queens, an atmosphere filled with danger and intrigue. A few newsmen have enjoyed the confidences of the truly great, but the majority meet more politicians than they do princes. Most reporters talk to all kinds of odd characters and see nothing very unusual in their material.

Indeed, newsmen are not unduly disturbed by the quirks of the human beings around them, nor, in the words of Bob Casey, ". . . should they be, for, of all the strangely contrived persons in the world, any number of puzzled critics will admit that they, themselves, are the strangest."

This is not to say that good reporters do not see the queer traits which distinguish people. They are aware of idiosyncracies. They know that their interviewees are people of only ephemeral importance. Always, the able reporter asks in the back of his mind, "What makes this guy click?" He keeps his curiosity about people alive. Human nature is an endless parade. The reporter watches it constantly. Why? Because it is the laboratory from which he obtains his material.

You may be a veteran fisherman, but you cannot predict in advance how many fish a particular trout-fly will catch. Why? You will never know enough about the fish.

Just so with people. Psychologists have been studying them for years. We have watched people's habits, added up the statistics, and reduced them to percentages. But we still don't know enough about them to predict their behavior with scientific accuracy. So for the next few paragraphs let's take a closer look at some of the complexities and dynamics which we will find in the interviewee's patterns of belief and behavior, and also in ourselves.

We Call It Human Nature

First of all, no two people are exactly alike. Simple as this fact seems, it is basic if we are to understand persons whom we interview. Not even identical twins, who resemble each other in many ways, are really identical. Each has certain characteristics which distinguish him from his twin. Stand on a busy corner and watch the throngs of people walking by. There is some sameness in dress or colors. Perhaps. But remember that no two of the people are alike. Some appear queer, quaint, or quizzical, but everybody is a somebody. And he is the only one of his kind in the world.

Every person, whether he is compelled as a prisoner of the Russians to work on the northern link of the Trans-Siberian railway or whether he lolls in the comfort and splendor of the Waldorf Astoria, is a bundle of attitudes. He has general attitudes toward classes of objects, people, and ideas. Some of them he has inherited, some have been obtained through generalizations made from a few experiences of a particular sort, and others absorbed from the general culture. Moreover, he possesses certain attitudes and tendencies that are individually unique.

Is your interviewee aware of his many attitudes? Yes, at times. He is conscious of and may even discuss his attitude toward the "Fair Deal," hot-check artists, juke boxes, communism, or his wife's cooking. Of other attitudes he is not conscious, or at least only intermittently conscious. At times he may be "all mixed up." William Albig in *Public Opinion* says, "That behavior is so frequently widely at variance with certain attitudes of the individual is not surprising, for on a given point he has many other attitudes in his attitude pattern."

Your interviewee is not always aware of the reasons for his conduct. This fact was emphasized by Edward L. Bernays when he said, "We don't tell the researcher that we buy punching bags to relieve our aggressions, or mirrors to gratify our narcissism, or a book on etiquette to improve our social status." Fundamentally, if we seek to know more about the art of interviewing, we must give more time to a deeper study of man and his behavior.

Let us look at a crucial concept which we sometimes

11

forget—the culture matrix. Our main conditioning factors come from our culture pattern, the environment in which we are born and grow up. About 90 per cent of the average man's behavior in any given society is automatically determined for him by the rules he begins to learn almost the moment he is born, Stuart Chase believes. And no matter where he goes— to a community picnic, a formal dance, a defense plant, or a poker game—he follows the behavior proper in that location.

Colonel Bluffington, whom you interviewed yesterday, is "set in his ways," you say. He isn't too different in some ways from millions of other people. As a matter of fact, very few people ever question their own evaluations. People hate to change their minds about anything. Usually they just say to themselves, "This is how I've always felt about things and that's the way I will always feel. Nothing can make me change my mind." They are rigid about their opinions and beliefs. Furthermore, they resent having to question and re-examine their attitudes. As an interviewer, you must remember that people resent having others criticize or question their attitudes.

You know persons who have filled their mental attics with junk. They have never had enough courage to take an inventory and decide what is worth saving, what is worth repairing, and what is to be tossed into the junk pile. Psychologically, it takes courage to admit that you have been wrong, to admit that you have been on the wrong track. Keep that trait of human nature in mind the next time you urge someone to do an "about face" in his views or beliefs.

You get as you bring. Psychologists who have probed deeply into human nature know that what you experience in a situation depends upon the likes and dislikes that you bring into it. What you experience depends upon how you look at things. Does your interviewee face his meeting with you with anxiety? Fear? Hopefulness? Doubt? Wonder? His negative feelings may come mainly from his own imagining. How can you rid him of this rigidity? In your approach and in your techniques, stress the factors which reduce inner conflicts and tension. Then the whole experience will be more pleasant and profitable for both of you.

Without a complete picture of the interviewee you will probably be astonished. A tough-looking fellow may turn out to be kind and co-operative. The business tycoon who calmly directs the affairs of a huge concern may be uncomfortable making a speech. The fellow who is rough and cocky in his press relations while seated behind his big desk in his own office may be uneasy and frightened when button-holed by reporters in the lobby of a hotel. The more situations in which you see a person, the more likely you are to see him as he is.

People may behave in the same way for entirely different reasons. At the next social gathering you attend, glance around and pick out several quiet people. One may be quiet because he is tired. Another may feel inferior and thus say nothing. Still a third may keep quiet because he feels superior and does not want to be a part of the group. People may also act in different ways, but for similar reasons. Any reporter can see the many and varied activities of men who are seeking political power within a community. Although they seek the same goal, their routes differ.

Here's What All Men Want

What do people strive for? What are their basic needs? Some people want big houses, approval from one person or another, security, or power.

Many psychologists have attempted to list basic needs, and there are almost as many lists as there are psychologists. Behind the things we want are certain driving forces, drives which generate action. If we hope to predict and control the behavior of interviewees, we must discover the more fundamental needs that everyone is attempting to satisfy. Drives are strong, persistent, and often impel us to act without thinking. These basic needs should be broad enough to include all human behavior in all cultures, at all ages, and at all times.

The basic need of all people is preserving and enriching what some psychologists term "the phenomenal self." Everyone wants to be proud of himself one way or another. Even such odd behavior as flag-pole sitting, wearing gaudy clothing, and going over Niagara Falls in a barrel becomes understandable, even predictable.

In each situation, note that each act of the individual is an attempt to preserve or fortify his concept of himself. First of all, the individual wants to remain alive and kicking. As a result, he spends a great deal of time and energy to keep himself physically intact. He seeks food, water, and air; he rests. Remember, however, that the physical self is not an end in itself. Mr. Average Man must also meet certain cultural demands. He could live in a cave on Little River and enjoy a variety of nourishing food, but his self-esteem would probably suffer. Living as a healthy hermit, he would lose his self-worth, his self-respect. He would suffer.

Every individual is tied strongly to his beliefs, his prejudices, his loves—every trait that makes up his personality. And he will stick with them. Hadley Cantril reminds us that "Unfortunately, the psychologist knows that many people have so identified themselves with their own group standards that they would, literally, rather die than give up their identifications." As an interviewer, you cannot toy with the values on which a man has built his life.

People are not robbers or law-abiding citizens, Republicans or Democrats, agnostics or devout believers, good or bad, because of innate dispositions. Consider your friends. They do not act as they do because they are blessed or cursed with a certain kind of "human nature." Rather, their actions take certain directions because a particular set of conditions has provided status, meaning, and satisfaction in that direction. In critical times they act as they do because status, meaning, and satisfaction must be sought in new ways.

To live and stay alive demands that man engage in a continuous process of adaptation to any and all environments in which he finds himself. R. R. Spencer calls attention to the fact that "Life for every individual is a one-way street; there are no U-turns." Birth, youth, maturity, senescence, and death are an inevitable biological sequence, an inviolate law of living nature.

In observing the gamut of human types, you are likely to believe that the objectives of persons seem widely diverse. One man wants a bigger pay check, so that his family will be cared for. Another seeks fame as a deep-sea diver, even if it means risking his life. Still another may turn evangelist and go out "to save the world." Yet behind these diverse objectives is a common goal: ego satisfaction.

Most human behavior is the result of mixed drives. We do not always eat, for instance, purely to satisfy our appetites. Nor do we usually play golf merely for the exercise. Every person, whether a debutante or a ditch-digger, has scores of drives operating simultaneously. What is more, these drives all flow into one another, generating widespread chemical and muscular changes. But only some of them reach proportions sufficient to give activity a specific character.

What happens to your drives when you get all mixed up, when you know that you can't have your cake and eat it, too? Not all drives reinforce each other. Some get in each other's way. Your interviewee, for instance, may want to tell you the truth, but to tell you the truth would bring humiliation to his friend. His drives clash.

Voting, buying an automatic washing machine, studying French, joining the Friends of the Friendless club— these are examples of broad tendencies, uniting so many separate drives that it may be impossible to disentangle any one from the whole.

Only as you understand with a person can you polish your interviewing techniques. This means that you must see the expressed idea and attitude from the other person's point of view, to sense how it feels to him, and to see how it has personal meaning for him. But that is not all. You must see how his attitude is combined with an emotional factor. Psychologically, you must achieve his frame of reference in regard to the subject he is talking about.

This is not easy. Don Hayakawa, the semanticist, has pointed out that real courage is required to enter the world of another person and see the way life appears to him. Courage is required because you run the risk of being changed yourself. You might find yourself influenced in your attitudes. You might be changed so that your individual world is threatened. Seek to understand people, not to judge them, and many of the barriers in your human relations will fade.

Try though you may, you cannot work out a sure-fire list of appeals which you can tap in motivating men. "Human motives," Professor Cantril reminds us, "are almost as numerous as men themselves, ranging from the comparatively simple desire for shelter or mate to the search for an all-embracing metaphysics or for the South Pole." To be sure, you may know about the fairly stable elements in the masses of people. But to understand the other person, you must study not only motives, but attitudes, sentiments, and other social factors making for consistency and inconsistency in what he says and does.

Attitudes Flick the Switch

It is an interesting fact that personal actions and beliefs may change greatly from cultural expectation through a change in a person's attitude toward himself. Thus the people of your town are shocked when J. D. Pennybacker, the bank cashier, is charged with embezzlement. You had respected him as an honest, trustworthy man. Nothing had changed in his duties or in the situation around him. What, then, had happened? For some reason or another, his concept of himself had changed. Perhaps he imagined that he was underpaid, unappreciated, or misunderstood. In all probability he had a feeling of inadequacy or failure.

Some people resist change. For example, the older a person grows, the more he is likely to become conservative. You say, "He is set in his ways." Haven't you noticed an elderly woman dressed in the style of several decades ago? The culture about her—styles, fads, and customs—underwent changes, but she remained about the same. Even though the demands made upon her by all of the subcultures—church, community, study club, family, or nation—changed, she continued to do the things which were "right" or "proper" forty years ago. As you see, the older the person, the more likely he is to remain rigid in his views and behavior.

What happens when a person's behavior passes the point of tolerance? Your friends can tolerate some differences from expected behavior, but you can't go too far from the expected. Mr. R. H. Corny, president of Crackie-Krunchie Cereals, for instance, proposes a new policy to his board of directors. The members of the board won't accept his proposal. Thus his need for satisfaction is frustrated. Inside he feels that "something is wrong." Naturally, he is unhappy and dissatisfied. In searching for satisfaction, he may try new goals, new techniques which will bring him better results. What happened here is obvious: When a person realizes that his activities do not give him satisfaction, he is likely to change them to others more likely to give results.

You Meet Them Every Day

Let's make the rounds on your news beat today and see how four persons illustrate some basic needs. Remember that these needs never arise by themselves, but always grow

17

out of specific situations. And, too, remember that some things man wants only temporarily—at noon, tomorrow night, or next Saturday; other things he wants throughout his life. Let's talk to some typical interviewees:

9:15 A.M.—Mrs. J. P. Tiffany, who is devoting most of her time to social climbing, tells you of her forthcoming party. You should be impressed at the V.I.P.'s who will attend, the luxurious setting of the country club, an orchestra which plays "divinely." Social recognition, prestige, power—these are her basic drives.

9:40 A.M.—Here's Mr. K. L. Meek. You discover that he is colorless, almost too shy to talk. He has wanted a promotion desperately, but has a fear that the boss would refuse his request. He plugs away at the same job day after day. Often he thinks of doing the same work for another firm, but that would be taking a risk. So he keeps on doing the job assigned to him. He can support his family, unmolested and unworried. Thus he has security, a feeling of safety.

10:10 A.M.—You drop by the police station and find a teen-age boy being questioned. While on his way to school, he ran over an elderly man. The kid was driving a "hot-rod" car. Why does he drive such a car? To show others that he is daring and courageous. His basic urge: adventure.

11:15 A.M.—Over at the courthouse you find the district judge sentencing a man to the penitentiary. You talk to the man. "I don't mind going to the pen," he says, "but I hate to bring this shame to my mom and dad." He wanted their love and understanding. He needed affection. His specific want: response.

Note that in each of the preceding examples, each person behaved in a way which was appropriate to his own picture of himself. On the surface, the objectives of the four persons seem widely diverse. And yet there is a common goal: ego satisfaction. Each person, as we have seen, wishes to preserve his personal integrity, to find and maintain a place in the world.

How each one follows a different road map toward a different destination lends variety to the work of writers. Goals may vary, directions may be great in number, and routes offer a variety of ways; you see many objectives and strategies. But no matter what the means, each person is satisfying his ego drive.

The desire to be recognized, to be important, is no superficial matter. Actually, every person is self-centered to a great degree. Even generous and self-sacrificing persons—who give and do not count the cost—obtain greater happiness ·in doing for others than for themselves.

William Steig, in his *About People,* has drawn in caricature the various masks and false fronts that many of us put on. Whatever disguise it is that we employ, we put it on with some purpose. Perhaps we wish to hide our real self and to win applause for a self that is not there. Or maybe we wish to make ourselves more impressive or tolerable to ourselves. In most cases, we wish to do both.

"I want to be someone" is our deepest cry. As Ben Hecht reminds us, "We clamor to acquire a meaning, to participate, however humbly, in the world of ideas and events; to hold opinions that will make us significant; to lift ourselves out of a herd-loneliness that eternally engulfs us."

It is a basic fact that every person is the center of his own universe; that is, as long as the roles he is called upon to play lead to the maintenance or enrichment of self, he will continue to act in a particular way. Whenever it becomes clear that his roles—his activities and interests—are inconsistent with his way of regarding himself, then he will change to others more likely to produce results.

How does the individual regard himself? is an important question for the interviewer. The man who regards himself as a fairly efficient mechanic probably does not set a goal for himself to be secretary of the United States Navy. Nor does a successful bank president adopt as a goal retirement to an easy job as night watchman in a factory. What goals are considered worth an individual's consideration are dependent upon the ways in which he regards himself.

Actually, the goals toward which an individual aspires—whether to become a snake charmer or an expert on jet planes—are determined by his ego satisfaction. Furthermore, if the person is realistic, his ambitions will be set on a plane possible for one of his abilities to achieve. He tells himself, "I've got what it takes to do so-and-so."

In gearing your interviewing techniques to this basic drive, you must be ready to show the person how he will benefit from the experience, how he will gain in prestige, power, courage, or self-satisfaction, or how much better he will be understood. William James, the Harvard psychologist declared, ". . . the deepest principle of human nature is the desire to be appreciated."

Insight Determines the Outlook

Now let's go a step further. We know that the interpretations you bring to anything that happens to you give that experience power to help or harm. Your interviewee, for instance, may experience joy or fear or rage when you are questioning him, depending upon the likes and dislikes which he brings into the situation. The outcome depends entirely upon his attitude, his evaluation.

This difference in ways of looking at things can mean happiness or unhappiness. There is the case of the woman who complained to a hotel manager, "Someone is pounding a piano in the next room. You'll have to make him stop. He's driving me crazy."

"I'm sorry, but I can't help you," the manager replied. "You see, that's Paderewski practicing for his concert tomorrow night."

Immediately the woman telephoned her friends, who came to sit with their ears to the wall. Her attitude was completely changed. The piano music had made her nervous until she found out that it was Paderewski. Then she became grateful and happy.

Let's dissect the anatomy of your interviewee's attitudes for a moment. Here is J. K. Bigdome. Whatever happens to him—in business, at his lodge meetings, or on a picnic with the church board—will be interpreted in accordance with his predispositions.

His likelihood of reacting a certain way includes his habits of evaluation, which are conditioned by his environment. Remember that his attitudes include the way he looks at things, the way he feels about them, and the way he is prepared to act. These three factors are interrelated. Each one influences the other two. Psychologists call this sort of arrangement a dynamic interrelationship.

By looking at Mr. Bigdome's attitudes from three sides, you have three possible levers with which to control them. First, find out the way he looks at things. Secondly, try to discover how he feels toward them. And then, if you know these two attitudes, you are likely to know how he will react under given circumstances.

Suppose Mr. Bigdome refuses to co-operate in an interview. What caused his reticence? All the forces working on him from his existence as an embryo to the time he did not respond to your questions provide the reasons. In other words, his failure to respond was not due to a single cause. Rather, his behavior was the result of many forces, most of which are unknowable.

An interviewer often assumes that if he could discover the one cause behind a respondent's failure to talk, there would be no further problems. Today most psychologists and psychiatrists believe that we should not isolate any single factor as the sole reason for a person's behavior. Rather, we should remember that behavior is the result of the interactions of millions of forces inside and outside the individual.

What can you do about the situation? Do some fact-finding. Stay out of blind alleys of the past. Take a good look at the attitudes. Then see what factors you can change in the interviewee. Ravel out some of the contributing factors and work on those which you can control.

Guideposts in Judging Personality

Let's take a look at the many-sidedness of your interviewee. You may find him:

Inconsistent. One day he likes a musical number, the next day he is repelled by it. One month he enjoys warm weather, the next month he wishes it were cold. Today he says, "I get a big kick out of my job." Tomorrow he hates it.

"Human." Often you read that "today's citizen is more cynical and more sophisticated than he was a few years ago." Maybe he is a bit disillusioned. Maybe it is harder to crack the shell of his personality. But he is still human enough to react to any antidote to defeatism, cynicism, fatalism, and what Norman Cousins terms "day-to-day-ism." His heart decides a lot of things for him.

A Poor Observer. Like all humans, your interviewee has an inclination to see what he wants to see. He believes that something is true if it fits into his scheme of things, if it brings him satisfaction. He interprets an event differently, not because he wants to distort the truth, but because he sees it in a different way from anyone else.

Swept Along by Fads. Whether it is chain letters, mah jong, or fox tails, a person is likely to be caught in the pressure of such goings-on. Few persons can resist the bandwagon appeal—"everybody's doing it."

A Dollar-Chaser. Why? Money talks. Almost every individual believes that the possession of wealth is evidence of worth. And, too, he is apt to imagine that with money he can buy happiness.

A Conformist. Man is a follower. What's more, he will avoid anything that might make him conspicuously different from other members of his group. He will heed the thousands of pressures brought to bear upon him—all tending to make him feel, look, and act like everybody else.

Restless. Since man conforms to the pattern of life about him—wise or foolish—he becomes crowd-minded. And then, bored with that type of existence, he shows a hysterical enthusiasm for sports or excitement—any activity which provides thrills. He tries to keep up with the Joneses without having any idea which way the Joneses are going.

Standardized. Man has lost his creative ingenuity. Thus he relies on what mass producers tell him is in the best taste. He is a sucker for new models. He belongs to the Novel-of-the-Month-Club, the Tune-of-the-Month-Club, the Vitamin-of-the-Month-Club, and the Fish-of-the-Month-Club. His possessions, his way of life, have become standardized.

A Spectator. It's easier just to watch. Mr. Average Citizen does not play games any more. He watches. He may see television, watch movies, and read endless mystery stories. Rather than step up his activities, he prefers to sit and take it easy. His only exercise is jumping at conclusions.

A Rationalizer. Mr. B. looks for excuses to do something he should not do. Actually, it's a convenient way of getting around his better self without seeming to do so. He kids himself. This device can be harmless, but when it involves the welfare of others, it may cause unhappiness.

Part Actor. From infancy every person learns to modify his expression, gestures, and tones in a manner similar to those around him. He must not wince when hurt. He must not throw a tantrum when angry. Then he finds out both when and how to show emotion. He learns to use the social smile, the raised eyebrows that go with disapproval, and the frigid tones of disgust. Most average adults seek to conceal their real emotion. That is because social pressure has taught them to submerge most emotions.

Lonely. Our society lays great emphasis on being socially accepted. It is our chief mark of prestige, Rollo May,

23

psychologist, says. Thus we have to prove we are a "social success" by being forever sought after and by never being alone. Indeed, if a person is alone very much of the time, people tend to think of him as a failure. So the average man becomes a "joiner" of all sorts of organizations.

A Grievance Collector. First of all, he feels sure that he is unlucky. Then he just knows that his boss discriminates against him, that his good work is unrewarded. He magnifies slights and injustices. He broods and utters, "No one appreciates me." And then he goes into heights of gloomy aloofness.

Ruled by Habits. Habit saves us the annoyance of making countless little decisions. Without them, of course, we would never get anything done. An old, time-tested habit eases the daily routine. Rather than attempt anything new, we keep doing the familiar things. Thus we conform to an established pattern of behavior.

Confused. Never has the average man been subjected to so many stimuli. Through the streamlined media of communication—the radio, television, motion pictures, the press, and others—he is urged to "make up his mind." A formidable battery of skilled persuasion is directed toward him from every side. Yet he can't decide. He is tragically confused.

Of course, any person may be a combination of these factors and still more. There is nothing fixed or static or immutable about human nature. Under new conditions any person may exhibit new and heretofore undreamed of possibilities and reactions. Mr. J. Phil Lucre, the shy office clerk, may surprise and even shock some of his associates by his dance of the seven veils at the annual employees' dinner of the Neverlock Zipper Corporation.

After all, each person—the ballet dancer and the bullfighter—must constantly adjust both his actions and his thoughts in keeping with his notion of "self." For this reason the preceding sidelights do not make a full-length portrait of man. But you may be sure of one thing: you can use them as guideposts in the evaluation of personality.

Always Build People Up

Do you build people up or tear them down? Not in your copy, but in the total impact of your personality. A city editor on a California newspaper was talking about his top-flight reporter: "You know Jim is a real newspaperman. He can write—he can do wonders with words. Best of all, people like Jim—his very presence builds you up."

To be sure, you may not like your job. You may detest your run. You are quite certain that your city editor is a slave-driver. And if you discuss these matters as a Prophet of Doom, then your news sources are less responsive. And you say, "I will just be a little Pollyanna and everything will be lovely."

No, that is not the idea. You do not need a psychological laboratory to see the dynamic effect of positive words on people. Which type of person attracts you: Mr. Sourpuss, who is always bewailing hard times, trouble, worry, and sickness; or Mr. Dynamic, who makes you feel important, happy, and responsive? All of your interviewees experience a certain emotional reaction when they see you and hear you talk. Use words and questions which lift people. You will feel better, your run will be more productive, you will find new drama in the commonplace, and, best of all, you will make friends and keep them.

You can make your interviewee feel important by remembering the personal side of his nature. If last week Dr. Seymour Tonsils said he hoped to lower his golf score in matches over the week end, ask him today how he came out in the tussle with par. If you have not seen him for a while, ask if he has been away and if he had a good time.

Remember that the best interviewing is sincere and highly personalized. And it depends to a great degree on the interviewee's opinion of you.

Watch For "About-Face" Changes

Have you ever been received cordially by an interviewee one day and the next day found him "up-in-the-air" about your treatment of the story? He knows you were correct, but he had hoped that your story might be more favorable toward him. Maybe he took a "friendly press" for granted—no matter what his actions or beliefs. When he sees that you and other newsmen have changed in the way you treat him, he no longer feels adequate and comfortable. Psychologically, his new perceptions are inacceptable in his old frame of reference. "That story in the morning papers," he explains to friends, "was really a blow to me."

Let's look a bit closer at this person. How does he deal with the situation? He may say to himself, "Oh, I'll just forget it, and the whole thing will soon blow over." Yet he probably realizes that this method is merely postponing a solution to the problem.

Or he may say, "It wasn't my fault." He knows, however, that he must face the same situation time and time again in the future, so he adds, "Oh, it's just one of those things. After all, the newspaper boys have been pretty nice to me so I'll have to 'play ball' with them."

There are so many variations in this kind of reaction that you will find it profitable to discover how any upset person re-establishes his feeling of self-esteem and adequacy. Many a powerful person, who may enjoy almost complete mastery of his surroundings, is often shaken when he discovers that he cannot influence reporters and editors. He may explode in anger. He may resort to physical force. In fact, he may set up a whole chain of aggressive reactions. He goes all to pieces because he has lost his feeling of self-assurance, power, and security. Ordinarily, however, he changes his attitude toward reporters. He obeys the adage, "If you can't lick 'em, join 'em."

Concentrate on the Individual

Can you predict how interviewees may react? Yes, to a certain degree. The more you know about psychology, the easier it will be to solve some of your problems in interviewing. Don't spend too much time in studying facts that are normative in nature. From these facts you may conclude that this person is likely to act this way in this particular situation. While it is true that the prediction of averages is useful in advertising research, marketing, and many other areas, such predictions are concerned with the behavior of the masses, not with that of one particular individual. In interviewing, prediction of normative behavior is not enough because you must deal with an individual. To predict his reaction to your techniques in questioning, you must do more than follow normative methods.

Perhaps you believe that you know what a normal or typical person will do in such a situation. But are you certain that the person you plan to interview is typical? Can you be sure that because something has happened so many times in the past, it will happen again in the future? Not exactly. Even psychologists are doubtful that individual behavior is ever repeated exactly.

If we are to observe Mr. Widgits' behavior, we must observe it from his point of view—how he looks at life from inside. So we ask, "What is he thinking? What does he want? How does he feel about this topic?" To Mr. Widgits, his behavior is purposeful. It always has a reason. Sometimes these reasons are vague and confused, and on other occasions they are extremely clear and definite. To you, his behavior may seem irrational. You must remember that he behaves in each situation the most effective way he knows how at that particular moment.

Caution: Don't "Type" People

If you aren't careful, you will fall into the practice of regarding all interviewees as stereotypes. It was a widely known newspaperman, Walter Lippmann, who popularized the use of the term "stereotype" to represent the predilection of people to pass judgment upon an individual on the basis of what is considered true of the group to which he belongs.

Actually, the newspaper helps perpetuate the stereotypes. You have noticed how a cartoonist creates a figure easily recognized as a Wall Street tycoon, a big-footed policeman, an absent-minded professor, or a monocled Englishman. Orientals are sly, Negroes are happy-go-lucky, reformers are pious and critical. No psychologist would agree with any of these generalizations. Like any other person, you face the difficulty of overcoming the stereotypes which you have acquired through the years. Somehow you must discover the uniqueness of each person to whom you talk.

In addition, you must watch your prejudices. According to Kimball Young, in *Social Psychology,* "A prejudice is an opinion or attitude, favorable or hostile, based on prepossession and therefore biased and irrational." As a human being, you possess certain prejudices. You acquired some of them from teachers and some from personal experience. Ordinarily, your boss, the editor, shares the prejudices of the community in which he operates. Try to stay above your personal prejudices. If you don't, you will find yourself irrational, and intolerant, and bigoted.

If you are prejudiced, you are likely to judge a person according to a fixed attitude and not on his individual merits or characteristics. Perhaps for some reason an industrialist has refused to grant you an interview. If you know him or agree with most of his ideas, you may ignore the incident. But if you know he is opposed to the policies of your newspaper, you may be inclined to say, "That's just like a big shot—playing hard to get."

Do First Impressions Count?

By this time you are probably asking, "Do first impressions mean much in judging another person?" "First impressions," explains Philip Eisenberg, "are sometimes correct, but they are usually not trustworthy. When people are transparent, or simple, or when they have no reason to be deceptive, they may give correct first impressions." He adds that most people have been schooled to convey a favorable impression rather than to give an honest picture of themselves. Thus the real person may often be successfully camouflaged.

Like most persons, you probably pride yourself on your ability to judge others. "There's a language in every gesture," Shakespeare wrote in *A Winter's Tale*. No matter how carefully one watches his words and facial expressions, his real feeling and thoughts often come through gestures, postures, and mannerisms. Your ability to read these telltale signs can give you short cuts to the interviewee's real self.

Have you ever noticed how a person's fundamental nature is clearly proclaimed in his habitual gestures? Remember the jaunty upward angle of F. D. R.'s cigarette holder—it showed his self-confidence. Generally, we express doubt, pessimism, dejection, disgust, and unhappiness in downward gestures. On the other hand, people usually reach or look upward and outward to express hope, faith, courage, fervor, and enthusiasm. If your news source makes inward gestures toward the body, he may be inhibited, cold, frightened, or worried. Forget your belief that shifty eyes mean a guilty conscience. It may be so in certain situations, but it is well to know that hardened criminals can control their eyes with brazen assurance.

This skill in appraising people from the outside

calls for practice and observation. Remember, too, that one gesture does not tell the whole story. Keep practicing, and your skill will increase. And as William B. Ziff reminds us, "You will be surprised to find that sometimes people can be heard better by looking at them than by listening to them."

It's the Mood that Matters

If you are to understand people, you must know something about their moods. Tune in on idle conversation and you will hear remarks which indicate various degrees of temperament. One person joyfully proclaims, "I'm as high as a kite." Another moans, "I'm really in the dumps." What causes these feelings of gladness or gloom? Can you predict elation or depression? You can to some extent if you know some of the conditions which influence moods. Look for these three:

Body condition. Whether the person feels "like a million dollars" or "lousy" affects his behavior. Poor physical condition may result in feelings of despondency, fear, or humiliation. If you feel blue—"in the dumps"—you are likely to feel tired. On the other hand, if you feel well physiologically, then you are more likely to feel competent, well adjusted, and poised. The main thing to remember is that this process works both ways: bodily conditions can affect behavior, and, conversely, emotions can bring about changes in bodily conditions.

Circumstances. Circumstances will affect your reception. Let's drop in mentally on your interviewee before you arrive. He may be in a state of indecision. "Shall I tell this reporter all of the facts? Shall I urge him to see Mr. Jackson because he is really the person who announces company policies? Would it be better if I postponed the interview? What if I say the wrong thing?" He may want to give you the information, but his fears hold him back.

Or suppose you call someone about a news story at two o'clock in the morning. He isn't too happy. Or you call during the dinner hour and the interviewee seems polite and yet a little disgusted. Psychologically, both men feel a sense of intrusion. Why? Your request clashes with two basic urges: food and rest. This does not mean that reporters must contact interviewees only at times convenient to the latter, but when a reporter must contact his interviewee at an unusual time, he should remember that he may be rebuffed because his source may regard the experience as undue intrusion.

General Outlook. If you know how a person looks at life—his philosophy—then you have a key to his attitudes and feelings. You must remember, also, that an interview may have different meanings for different people. How a person reacts is influenced by the nature of the experience, his age, previous life experience and personality development, and the timing of the specific interview in relation to the other events of his life. Always consider all ingredients which the person has blended into his philosophy of life.

Obviously, your interviewee's behavior is influenced by countless other factors, even those of a hereditary nature. How he reacts to you at a particular time under certain specific conditions is the result of the interaction of many elements. No matter what the cause of emotional patterns in the interviewee, you should strive to see his behavior as it appears to him.

Read! Observe! Listen!

Are you as a writer keeping alive your curiosity about people? One way to do so is to observe what psychologists term "uncontrolled behavior situations." Watch people enjoying a swim at the beach, streaming from the theater, attending the county fair, or in any of a hundred other situations not under the direct control of the observer. Be alive to the meanings which make people act as they do, and you will gain added insight into individual behavior.

You ended your interview with Mr. Smalltalk the other day when he kept glancing at his watch. You knew it was time to conclude your visit. That is a simple example of how we strengthen our knowledge of human nature by observing behavior. In other words, we are constantly modifying our behavior as we make judgments of what others like or dislike. Caution: Watch the other person's acts in terms of their meanings for him. Ask yourself, "How would one have to feel to act like that?"

Listen in on conversations of others—on trains, planes, in super markets and coffeeshops, and at your lodge meetings. Much of what you hear is small talk. But always remember that an individual's remarks about other people and events are likely to be a projection of his own feelings and attitudes. If you want to improve your psychological know-how, then be aware of the deeper meanings of conversation.

Steep yourself in current books and magazine articles on psychology. By gaining a knowledge of this science, you will understand better some of the hidden forces which make people act as they do. Psychology will help you to see the wide range of individual differences, together with the "average" or "typical" level of performance to be expected from large groups. When you are dealing with education, intelligence, ambitions, hates, loves—everything involved in emotional make-up—these differences are great.

Through psychology you can find explanations of many of the phenomena of human behavior—association, attention, interest, suggestion, and identification. By understanding these traits, you can predict interviewee reactions and responses with greater ease.

But, you may say, "While psychology is an excellent study, it deals largely in intangibles. How can it help me as an interviewer?" It is true that many of the leads offered by psychology cannot be exact, but only comparative, but you should not forget that these indicators are significant.

Of course, even correct use of psychology is not enough. Equally important is the personality and judgment and news sense of the reporter. After all, it is the skill which the reporter uses in combining many varied elements which strengthens his proficiency in the art of interviewing.

You are subject to limitations of emotional characteristics just as your interviewee is. You must overcome your natural tendency to hear and write only those facts and opinions which harmonize with your own, while failing to note exceptions. If you want to keep all channels between you and the interviewee open, you will never put up emotional barriers in the situation. You must be extremely careful not to become emotionally involved and then form a judgment based on your way of thinking.

"If I understand the thoughts and feelings of other persons, does that mean more success in interviewing?" you may well ask. Not necessarily. You must see the world through the interviewee's eyes. Heed the advice of Carl R. Rogers, University of Chicago psychologist: "Listen with understanding." You might even find that people can be predictable!

3
Don't Depend on Luck

In PLAYING A GAME OF CHESS, you want to gain certain specific goals, and yet you must anticipate your opponent's moves. Not just his next move, but all plays until the end of the game. One wrong move on your part, and your adversary gains an advantage. Like chess, the art of interviewing demands the ability to concentrate on the present and at the same time to foresee what may happen in future maneuvers. You must be able to listen intently. You must be able to outguess the interviewee at times. If you are good, you can take specific statements and see how they fit into the picture as a whole. In your exploration of the respondent's thoughts and attitudes, you are leading the way. You steer clear of pitfalls which might end the interview. At all times, you guide the interview so that it has both balance and perspective.

What makes an interview click? First of all, the whole process depends upon countless factors—tangible and intangible. Particularly important is the mood of the interviewee. Perhaps he is worried and cannot concentrate. Maybe he is suspicious of all reporters. He may remember how the statements of a friend were garbled by a newsman. He may be nervous and incoherent. Perhaps the whole affair is too rushed. In this case the interviewee does not have time to adjust his mental set to the condition. Actually, there is no way by which the interviewee's attitude toward the reporter at a specific time can be predicted. But you can always help the situation by checking some factors in advance.

Put your creative power to work on your next assignment. If time permits, give your thoughts time for incubation. Perhaps you can't quite equal Mark Twain in using your imagination in creative planning, but you can try. "I use the meridians of longitude and parallels of latitude for a seine," said he, "and drag the Atlantic Ocean for whales. I scratch my head with the lightning and purr myself to sleep with the thunder."

One successful feature writer told me, "Before setting out to interview a person, I have sat in a chair and imagined my way through the entire problem from the first contact to the successful finish." Guided imagining helped him to become more proficient in interviewing.

You ask, "Is there a fixed approach?" Not at all. Nor can ten easy "do-it-yourself" lessons in successful interviewing be outlined. Too many factors are involved: the emotional climate of the meeting, attitudes, feelings, facts, likes and dislikes, whims, foibles, and so on. But you can use a pre-check list and thus avoid some of the pitfalls in interviewing practices. Here is a helpful list of basic principles that will raise the effectiveness of your efforts:

1. *"When in Rome . . ."*

Human beings are naturally gregarious. We want to be with people. We want them to like us. One of the surest ways of getting the other person to like you is to respect his way of life. This means adaptability. You won't interview Lord Bottomsley attired in your sport shirt. Nor will you overdress when you interview several elderly couples who have been evicted from an apartment house because of failure to pay the rent. The old folks may be drinking coffee from a sidewalk stove and offer you a cup. To refuse might reflect on the hospitality of the group. So attune yourself to the interviewee—his ideas, his customs, his beliefs, and his way of life.

2. *Remember the reader.*

In planning your questions, always ask yourself, "What would my readers ask if they had a chance to talk to this person? What would they like to know about him?" You are interviewing a scientist. His views are newsworthy, but so are the facts that he likes apple pie, plays bridge once a week, wears an old pair of corduroy trousers when writing his research papers, hates salesmen who ask, "Is that all to-day?," and will walk a mile to hear a "hoe-down" fiddler. Look for the human side. Here are some topics to remember in your approach to the interviewee: work, inter-personal relations, special interests, background, future, beliefs and convictions, and anecdotal material. Remember the reader— he is the third person in every interviewing situation.

3. *Know all you can about your interviewee.*

Careful preparation always pays off. If time permits, use all available sources to secure information about the person with whom you are going to talk. Read the clip files in the office, talk with the man's acquaintances, look up his connections, check biographical reference books, talk with other staff members—use all possible sources. Nelson Antrim Crawford tells of a reporter who became perplexed over a religious story, so much so that he attempted to look up Mary Magdalene in *Who's Who in America*. Only by knowing the person can you gear your questions to his way of life. Isaac F. Marcosson once said, "The whole trick in big interviewing is to know all about your subject before you see him."

4. *Make an appointment.*

By making an appointment, you will save time by seeing the interviewee promptly and by shortening preliminary explanations. Too, it is the courteous thing to do. You can arrange for the interview by telephone, by note, by using a letter of introduction from a friend, or in other ways. If a near deadline is approaching, then you must speed up the whole process. By having an appointment, you can map your strategy for a certain amount of time. Furthermore, you know that the hour is satisfactory to the interviewee.

5. *Arrange for privacy.*

Your interviewee will be more "at home" at his office, near his fireside, in his boat, or in any location where he spends a great deal of his time. Your interview may best be carried out in Mr. B.'s office because he may need to check certain material on file there. When personal information is sought, the presence of other persons is almost always inhibitory. Avoid "springing" questions on a man when he is standing with a group of friends in a hotel lobby, for instance. He is likely to be extremely cautious and may say nothing of interest. If you encounter him in a public place, it is much better to introduce yourself (if you have never met him) and ask if you may see him privately for a moment. Then, by walking even a short distance from the group, you and your interviewee can get down to business. The place and environment in which the interview takes place must, of course, be governed by the nature of the interview.

6. *Know all you can about the topic.*

Two factors can make or break the interview for you. One is your ability to guide and direct the conversation into the desired news channels. The second is your knowledge of the subject of the interview; indeed, the success of your efforts is likely to be in direct proportion to your knowledge of the subject. If you don't know the subject well enough, the interviewee may fear that he will be misquoted. Or, worse, he may feel that he is wasting his time. One show of ignorance on your part, and the interviewee may become reticent. "However well informed and gifted the interviewee, there can be no great interview without an able and alert interviewer," comments Edward Price Bell.

7. *Write out your questions.*

Only the cub reporter would say to himself, "Oh, I'll think of some questions as we talk." There may be little chance to do so. The interviewee may talk with the speed and sputter of a machine gun. Or he may use a protective armor against the questions of newsmen. Most likely of all, the interviewee may want to be helpful but not know what to say. He depends upon the reporter for prompting and ideas. If you fail to plan your questions, the outcome is likely to be confusion and very little copy, maybe two paragraphs hidden somewhere inside the paper. Plan your questions with care.

You should have a plan for the interview. Define your objective. What facts must be brought out, what information given, what attitudes established, what action motivated? Will the interviewee wish to reveal the facts? Will you be able to make clear exactly what information you want? Is the person prejudiced? Is he accustomed to talking to reporters? Use these and other questions as guides in formulating your queries. They will help you get the replies you need for a bright story.

8. *Be ready for negatives.*

Perhaps you have imagined that your interviewee will talk readily, but you discover that he has a complete armor of silence or that he harbors certain negative reactions. Ideally, you should be ready to change these negative reactions into positive ones. Suppose your interviewee takes one of the following attitudes:

"I don't want to be bothered."

"My opinions may seem ridiculous to others."

"I don't want to make any enemies, so I'd better keep quiet."

"After all, the incident didn't amount to much."

"If what I say is printed, it becomes a permanent record."

"Anyone would have done what I did under the same circumstances."

"It may come out garbled and that would be terrible."

On more than one occasion, you must convince someone that you need his co-operation. If you have any reason to believe that information will be refused, it is often wise to remove or state all of the objections before you ask a question. For example, in interviewing a doctor, whose professional code does not permit him to give information about a patient, it might be well for you to show that you are aware of professional ethics. Explain that you appreciate his position, "but here is the problem." Maybe he can help.

9. *Plan several approaches.*

You will find your job easier if you "mentally build one or more possible approaches," to use the words of Carl Warren, former Washington correspondent for the *Chicago Tribune*. After considering several plans of attack, outline definite questions which will focus the facts or comments you are seeking. As the interview gets underway, you can try one of the strategies and see what happens. If your interviewee is as silent as a wooden Indian, try another of your planned approaches. Then if nothing happens, use your next method. Ordinarily, if you have developed enough angles, enough plans of attack, the person will respond.

10. *Plan the possible angles from the topic to be discussed.*

If you know enough about your interviewee and his opinions and beliefs, you can guess approximately what he will say. Here is an eminent educator who believes very strongly that visual aids should not replace books in classrooms. What are the unique values of reading? Does he think that many of the modern visual aids provide more entertainment than information? What must teachers do to encourage students to read more? What are the limitations of films, slides, and other visual aids? How can stories from books be dramatized by the students? Should students be required to prepare more of their assignments at home? By planning your questions on various angles of the projected interview, you are better prepared to guide the conversation.

11. *Speak the language of the interviewee.*

Interviewing is communication—communication between persons. Psychologically, the interviewer's task has three aspects: the cues (or stimuli) transmitted by the communicator, the responses made by the communicatee or interviewee, and the laws and principles relating to these two classes of events. In other words, vocabulary research should be a definite part of your preparation. Then you can speak the language of those whom you are interviewing. Never talk down to them; never talk up to them; talk directly to them as much as possible.

Word your questions with care. Words have different connotations under different circumstances. The word "wolf" does not have the same meaning for a man in the Colorado wilds as it has for the penthouse dweller on Fifth

Avenue. Some words set loose strong emotions. Words become distorted. Sometimes they get stereotyped. To sum it up, express yourself in terms of the other person's vocabulary and in terms of his interests.

12. *Be ready to check results or figures with other sources.*

Suppose a prominent advertising executive comes to town and in an interview relates some recent findings in public opinion studies regarding advertising. He tells you that 71 per cent of the persons interviewed get helpful suggestions out of advertising; 58 per cent, new ideas; 50 per cent, information; and nearly 47 per cent, price information. Furthermore, he says that 54 per cent thought most advertising tries to play too much on consumer emotions. Testimonial advertising was condemned as a racket by 68 per cent. He concludes by saying that 41 per cent believed that half or more advertising is misleading. Then he adds, "Now I believe I'm correct in most of these figures, but maybe you'd better check them." You ask, "Who made the survey?" and he replies that he believes it was originally titled "Wage Earner Forum" and was made by the MacFadden Publications, Inc. You thank him and dash back to the office to check with your advertising manager. If he doesn't have the report, you must check with an advertising agency, a radio station, a direct-mail agency, or any source that might have a copy of the findings. Of course, you must check every possible source before writing your story. If you cannot locate the report, all you can do is to write the story and attribute the remarks and figures to the speaker. Neil MacNeil of the *New York Times* warns that "The reporter who believes all that he is told will not last long. The competent reporter takes all the data he can get. He may ask embarrassing questions. He checks one person's statement against another's and against the known facts. . . . He makes certain that he has exhausted all available information before he writes a word of his story."

12. *Know the age of the interviewee.*

One of the mental fences you'll have to climb over to get closer to your informant is age. An older person, for instance, is usually conservative or "set in his ways." The adolescent may be confused and bewildered. He is shy, but may talk boldly to hide inner doubts and fears. There is the child who says nothing in the presence of a stranger. Remember that the age of the person may be a vital factor in the success of the interview. By knowing his age, you may put the informant at ease, keep him talking freely, guide the conversation into the desired paths, and in other ways make the interview more resultful. Without being a psychologist, you must also be able quickly to estimate a person's mental age. Thus you can treat the person as emotionally mature or as an emotional child.

14. *Plan to make the most of the situation— expect results.*

A reporter complained, "I get all of the screw-ball interview assignments. I'm fed up with talking to emotional cripples and misfits. You can't like them. I just can't get enthusiastic about talking to them." Perhaps he was justified, but if he carries that attitude with him, he isn't likely to get much of a story. You can't just be an actor and say to yourself, "I'll really be happy in this interview." That won't work. You must fire your enthusiasm with a deep personal belief; you have to be thoroughly sold on the forthcoming experience. Reporters are often bitten by the bugs of boredom and sophistication. Don't let them get you!

How can you generate self-interest in that next assignment? First, have a goal. Because intent and interest are strengthened when you set up an objective. Secondly, keep your eyes and ears wide open—be aware of things about you. Then by virtue of your awareness, you will develop the amazing power to see drama in the commonplace.

15. *Study the situation upon which the interview is based.*

Let's remember that every situation has objective and subjective aspects. A man loses an election. That is an objective fact. Yet his feelings about this defeat constitute a subjective aspect. One of the keys to successful interviewing is to use vicarious imagination in putting yourself in the other fellow's place—even to jotting down what your feelings might be if you were placed in the same situation. The movie actress from Hollywood usually welcomes an interview. That's easy. But your next assignment is to see a public official who is likely to present an exaggerated or false picture of the situation rather than give you the truth. Why does he want to hide some of the facts? Why does he withhold certain information? Those and other questions occur to you as you work and dig for new facts, new angles, interesting points, and colorful features.

16. *Anticipate the interviewee's mood.*

"Sometimes I'se up and sometimes I'se down, Oh, yes, Lawd." Such are the words of the old spiritual, and they are psychologically sound. You hope, of course, to catch the interviewee "up." If he was misquoted in Milwaukee yesterday, he may be in a sour mood when you call for an appointment to see him in Kansas City today. Perhaps your assignment is to interview a noted personage like Stokowski, who has what editors call a natural "news sense" and a shrewd feeling for the kind of story the editor is likely to use. Many times, of course, you cannot predict with any certainty how your informant will feel. Nor could a dyed-in-the-wool psychologist foretell just what will happen. Know the personality of the informant, consider the circumstances, plan strategies which will make the other person responsive, and hope for the best.

17. *Remember the time factor.*

If you know in advance how much time is to be allotted for the interview, you can make all plans—including the number and types of questions to be asked—with more efficiency. When the interviewee knows that his meeting with the reporter will terminate at a definite time, he also may organize his material and comments and present them more concisely. Many factors, of course, govern the length of an interview: the amount of time the interviewee (and sometimes the reporter) has at his disposal, the topic to be discussed, and the time it takes to establish a mutual feeling of confidence between the reporter and the interviewee. While no rules can be laid down for the length of the ideal interview, it is well to remember that a long interview, that exhausts both reporter and informant, is to be avoided when possible, as is the on-the-run interview except in cases of emergency.

Consider also the time of day at which the interview takes place, for it may affect the response of the interviewee. If you are a reporter for an afternoon paper, for example, you may often have to interview a celebrity at mid-morning after he has had only a few hours of sleep. Here, again, item No. 4—making an appointment—becomes important, for by so doing, you know that the time is convenient for the informant and that you are likely to obtain the best response.

18. *Remove all guesswork possible.*

Promise yourself that you will remember all the boners of past interviews and that you won't repeat them. Then decide upon some strategies and techniques which you have used with success. The bright boys and girls are those who have discovered that a lot of time and tears can be saved by a consistent attempt to do the best possible job. This means a thorough preparation in all fundamentals before you go into the interview. It means that you're going to start the interview prepared, alert, and ready with tentative strategies if the interviewee gets off the track, becomes angry, refuses to talk, or makes an unexpected move. If you've studied the facts, the person, and the situation, made allowances for unforeseen behavior, and tried to prepare all of the other ingredients which make a successful interview, you may be surprised how smoothly and how productive the experience can be for you.

19. *You come second.*

As a writer you should resolve that you will interview, not to be impressive, but to be understood. The success of the interview rests with you. In some cases the informant will await your coming with anticipation and pleasure, but most of the time, you cannot assume that the interviewee is greatly interested in you or your mission. That is why you must plan some way of catching and holding the attention and interest of the informant. Concentrate on the interviewee when you make your plans. Finally, challenge your strategies for credibility, interest, sequence, reaction, and response.

20. *Be prepared to accept the facts and other data professionally.*

As a writer, you will hear many statements and ideas—some bizarre, some amusing, many tragic. Ordinarily,

45

it is best not to portray surprise, shock, or emotional tension at any disclosures. On many occasions, you cannot show sentimental sympathy or antipathy. Feelings of boredom and disapproval must be absent. A city editor once advised me to "be tolerant and reasonable." As a professional writer, you must overcome your natural tendency to hear and record whatever harmonizes with your own philosophy, while failing to notice exceptions. Only by eliminating your own bias and prejudice and remaining largely impersonal can you write and interpret facts and comments professionally.

21. *Find the key which unlocks the other's personality.*

When Lord Kitchener, gruff, forbidding, and uncommunicative, arrived in the United States on his way back to England from India, he refused to be interviewed or photographed. "A soldier should keep his own counsel," he sternly informed the reporters.

But Nate Meissler, a well-known newspaper photographer, was not the sort of fellow who would calmly accept such a brush-off, Andrew Meredith relates in *Your Life*. Casting aside his usual polished, urbane manner, Meissler, a fat, roly-poly little figure of a man, deliberately made himself ridiculous by waddling after the famous Englishman and calling out in a plaintive voice, "Lord! Lord! Oh, my Lord! Oh, dear Lord! Just a minute, Lord!" The result? Kitchener smiled, then literally shook. "That's no way to address a lord," a fellow-reporter admonished Meissler. "You should have called him 'your lordship.'" "Lordship my eye," Meissler answered. "What's the difference what I called him —I got four plates." And that is how an enterprising photographer obtained the only laughing pictures of Lord Kitchener in all the world.

To find this key to more successful interviewing, you must know how the person behaves and thinks. More than that, you must know why the interviewee behaves and thinks as he does. What kinds of thoughts does he think? What prompts those thoughts? What does he want in life? What emotional stimulus can bring about the desired response? Adler said that on an oak tree there were no two leaves exactly alike. And in all the world there can never be two people exactly alike. Therefore, in your tentative approaches, you must not guess. You must know—you must base your strategy on the facts, opinions, and other information peculiar and germane to the specific situation. Dig hard enough, and you will find the magic key. With it, you can establish a common meeting ground; you can arrest the interviewee's attention and interest. Then he will respond in the desired way.

22. *Expect the unexpected.*

Interviews, like football games, are often won by planned strategies—strategies which are pin-pointed weeks, days, and hours before the event. And like the quarterback who calls the signals, you must size up the situation beforehand in terms of what is likely to happen—even zany, unpredictable reactions.

You must dig for every clue which will help you in sizing up your interviewee. Can you crash through his indifference, his fear, his reticence? You will have to muster enough strategies to turn objections into positive responses. And like a smart quarterback, you will mix your strategies. But always you will hold some of your most evocative and provocative ideas in reserve, just in case. For anything can happen in an interview. If you can anticipate the next move on the part of your interviewee, if you can stay one jump ahead of him, then you are "mobile"—to borrow a word from football coaches—and you will stay on the first team!

4
Ways to Win the Interviewee

IF ANYONE needs a multiple personality, it is the interviewer. He must be a diplomat, psychiatrist, writer, salesman, quiz master, confidante, scholar, and an expert in human relations. He is supposed to be an authority on everything from nuclear physics to Tommy Manville's bride-to-be.

That's not all. He must have a change of pace that makes big-league pitchers look like amateurs. One moment he uses the sweet, mellow personality and charms his subject. In the next interviewing situation he must act just as confident and talk just as big as his cocky respondent. He meets the daffy and the disillusioned. He can keep his balance only if he has the constitution of Gargantua and the quick wits of an ad lib comedian.

The top-flight interviewer needs more than skills and abilities. In the words of Max K. Gilstrap, chief of the Chicago Central News Bureau of the *Christian Science Monitor,* "The manner in which he does his job—his élan, long-headedness in concentrating on those things that are important—his insatiable inquisitiveness—and appearance of being on top of a job which he does with a flair, will be the things that pay off in the best reporting—and eventual promotion to the front ranks for enlarged service."

That the outcome of the interview rests squarely with the reporter is the belief of Mary B. Mullett, former staff writer for the *American Magazine:* "If you can stir the interest of the man you want to interview, if you are intensely alert to seize every opening and develop it, if you can not only interpret the man but can interpret him to himself, so that he will realize his 'drama' and be stirred by it, if you can ask intelligent questions . . . if you can make him sense the fact that you are reliable, accurate, and capable, well, with these few essentials you will get your material."

It is quite evident that what happens in a particular place, at a particular time, between two persons under certain conditions cannot be duplicated. In getting a good look at interviewing techniques, therefore, you must look at the conditions under which something happened and under which something did not happen. Basic principles, you see, can be established only when all variables are isolated or canceled out.

After all is said and done, you cannot depend upon formalized procedures. In his book, *Clinical Psychology,* L. E. Bisch, after advising his readers not to follow a method in a slavish, imitative fashion, says that "Understanding, foresight, and a full measure of old-fashioned common sense are essentials for worth-while results." He takes it for granted that the interviewer has the necessary facts, sound concepts, and psychological principles.

Let's take a swing around and look at many of the variables which pop up in interviewing. Why? Mainly because we can pin-point some strategies which result in successful interviewing. Yesterday's methods may flop today. What you hope people will do and what they actually do are two different things.

Watch Your Approach

Getting to see the right person may be your biggest problem. Reporter and columnist Dorothy Thompson got her first interview on what the trade calls "speculation." In Paris and broke, Miss Thompson asked every editor for a job. She kept herself in coffee and brioche by writing publicity stories for the Red Cross at one cent a line. Finally, she persuaded Wythe Williams, European editor for the Curtis newspapers, to let her have a try at Vienna.

She landed a world scoop shortly after the first world war by getting into the castle where the Hapsburg King Karl, pretender to the throne of Hungary, was a prisoner. Other correspondents were besieging the Foreign Office in Budapest for permits to interview the King. They were all refused.

Dorothy didn't go near the Foreign Office. Instead, she used her Red Cross connections and got into the castle in her nurse's uniform, talked to the King, and smuggled her interview into Vienna in a railway porter's pocket. Shortly after this the Curtis organization put her on the pay roll. She had dared to do the unusual and won!

J. R. Sprague, who has written articles for trade magazines, does not use the word "interview" in approaching businessmen. He merely tells the informant that he is seeking information on a certain subject and thus prevents the interviewee from becoming either reticent or unduly excited. And he never notifies a businessman that he is coming, because, as Mr. Sprague says, "He would either be embarrassed at the idea and shut up like a clam, or he would rise to the occasion and give an imitation of a speech he heard someone else make at the last convention." His secret: he keeps the whole interview on a natural and informal basis.

Your approach need not be perfect in order for you to gain an interview. William J. Reilly, authority on human relations, tells us that "all you have to do is to show a person that it is to his advantage to do what you want him to do—that the advantages of following your suggestion overbalance whatever disadvantages there may be."

Never telephone the interviewee and ask, "May I

see you today?" but "What time may I see you, at two o'clock or at three?" In your approach, use words which take for granted that your respondent does want to do what you suggest. Remember the Elmer Wheeler principle: Always give the person a choice between something and something, not between something and nothing.

To make the right approach: Remember that ingenuity is the self-starter which sets the interview in motion.

Accentuate the Positive

What will be the interviewee's first reaction to you? He may say to himself, "Now just what does this snooper want?" Or he may say, "Gosh, I really like this guy!"

In many situations his first reaction to you is distrust. Your total impact means a lot, and your looks are important. As Twila Neely reported in *A Study of the Error in the Interview,* most successful interviews were obtained by mature-looking, "reliable" persons, and a youthful appearance or an immature manner is a handicap that has to be overcome by interviewing skill.

First, sell yourself on the importance of the interview, and you will feel and act more confident. Avoid speaking hurriedly and nervously (anyone who lacks self-confidence nearly always talks fast). Feel sure of yourself. It will give you a deep-inside feeling of poise and charm. In the second place, give your interviewee the incentives which evoke co-operation. Jack up his ego. Remember: No one is interested in your idea until you arouse that interest. Do everything possible to build an atmosphere of co-operation.

"If you would win a man to your cause," said Abraham Lincoln, "you must first convince him that you are his sincere friend." Luckily, there is no secret about how to be well liked. If you sincerely want to be liked, it is not hard at all. We still like to do things for people we like. So does your interviewee.

One way of putting the other person at ease is to break the ice. How this can be done depends upon the personalities, the situation, and other factors. Will Rogers had this ability to a marked degree. Once Mr. Rogers, after standing in line at a presidential reception at the White House, finally reached President Calvin Coolidge and whispered, "My name is Will Rogers. What's yours?"

When we really like a person, we tend to minimize his faults and magnify his good points. When we dislike him, just the opposite is true. Recognizing this trait in human nature, if you want to make people like you, make a positive impression.

Summed up, one big secret of getting along with the interviewee almost instantly is *make him like you.*

Cheer Changes Things

Can you laugh at yourself? Do you have a sense of humor? You'd better have, because it will save situations and it will save you. To have a sense of humor does not mean that you must try to say something funny ever so often during the interview. Rather, it means that you must have an agreeable, pleasant frame of mind which will cause others to enjoy your presence and your conversation.

With a sense of humor, you can laugh at your own foibles and frailties. You won't be pompous and conceited. You won't "blow your top" when someone refuses to make any comment. You won't get disgusted and quit. You will place first things first. You won't "boil" inside. And if a heated discussion is approaching, as Herbert V. Prochnow reminds us, "you can often use a humorous observation on some phase of the problem, the tension is relieved, and there follows a calm analysis of the situation."

In addition, you won't carry sad tidings—you won't be a Prophet of Doom. People have troubles of their own and don't want to be reminded of them by hearing about yours. They want escape from their troubles.

Nothing can take the place of a friendly smile in building up people. Many veteran reporters maintain that a big, friendly smile is one of the most active agents in getting information from all types of persons, even the reticent and the hard-boiled. Theodore Roosevelt's great popularity was attributed to his ability to "beam all over" and be "dee-lighted" as he greeted each farmer and shoemaker as a long-lost friend. This indefinable charm, this compelling likability cannot be synthetic. It springs from a genuine interest in people.

Remember: He who laughs, lasts.

Breaking Down Barriers

Yes, you will be rebuffed by some of your news sources. When this happens, instead of thinking, "This person is a pretty tough cookie, and one of these days I'm going to really tell him a thing or two," ask yourself, "Am I doing something which causes him to put up his mental fists every time he sees me?" Sometimes you discover that what you are getting is nothing more than a mirror reflection of what you are giving.

You must recognize, just as the doctor and the psychiatrist, that anger, antagonism, non-co-operation, indifference, and reticence are not in themselves wrong—they are symptoms. "What is the basis of his feeling toward me?" "How can I rid him of the symptom and thus get the response

I am seeking?" By finding the answer to these questions, you may find the proper key of persuasion.

Never believe for a moment that all interviewees will welcome you with open arms. Some of them may try to insult you. For reasons that psychologists have never revealed, certain individuals who are ordinarily polite and courteous regard a reporter as someone to be abused. On rare occasions you may use a penetrating phrase to deflate the egocentric. Generally it is best to ignore the discourtesies and proceed directly with the questioning.

Whatever the resistance, the interviewer must transfer it from its usual place of working against him to the side where it will work for him.

> So . . . make it easier for the interviewee to talk than to keep quiet.

Walk into His World

You may think that you and your interviewee are "miles apart." Indeed, your ideals, concepts, activities, sentiments, and traditions which do not lie within the culture of the interviewee may be misconstrued and bring about highly incongruous results.

Knud Rasmussen interviewed Eskimos whose language and customs were familiar to him, yet he could not quite make himself understood, he relates in *Across Arctic America*. Upon one occasion he tried to explain to an Eskimo that he was interviewing him on behalf of a daily newspaper. He tried to tell him that all that passed between them would be made known to people through the medium of the "talkmarks" which the native had seen him making in his notebook. Furthermore, Rasmussen said, what they talked about would be printed on sheets of fine "skin" so that men could learn what was happening each day. The Eskimo chuckled. He regarded this as a witticism. The world of the white men was big, yet it could not be so big that a man might not learn all the news there was by inquiring at the nearest tent. The men were out of step with each other. There can be no interview if you and the subject don't talk the same language.

To be successful as an interviewer, you must establish what the French call *rapport*—a relationship characterized by harmony and accord. To establish such an atmosphere, you must accept the interviewee for what he is rather than for his status. This means that you must be able to adapt your actions to varied types of persons. Here are some tips for creating the desired atmosphere:

Use opening remarks which interest him—if the two of you have a mutual friend, you can say, "Duncan Strayer sends you his best regards."

Avoid thrusting big questions too early in the interview.

Accept the other person as your conversational equal.

Observe the conventionalities which he sets up.

Eliminate social distance, when possible.

Do not make tactless remarks.

Be alert enough to find something about his manner, life, experience, or beliefs which you can conscientiously admire.

Accept things from his angle.

Hunt for the key which will unlock his castle of dreams.

How to Master Problem Types

Here are some people you will meet and some pointers for handling them:

The Gruff Fire-eater. Keep calm—don't let him frighten you. His grouchy exterior is probably a defense mechanism to keep him from being a pushover.

The Cocksure Fellow. Don't try to penetrate his resistance by beating it down. The more force you employ to put your ideas across, the more resistance he will summon. Go around his resistance by discussion. Agree on minor points, and you may get comments on major ones.

Mr. Wishy-Washy. Be patient. Avoid high pressure. Be understanding. Ask his objections. Steer him gently into desired channels.

"I'll Ask My Adviser." Sooner or later you will interview someone who relies heavily on the advice of someone else. You talk to two persons at once. Often the adviser, even without any past experience in talking to reporters, has strong opinions. If this is the case, you must win the confidence of both persons. Point out the advantages of the results. Do it tactfully, so that both the wavering interviewee and his friend will respond to your strategies.

The Timid Soul. Above all, don't rush him. Help him all you can. Assure him that he is making the decision. Ask his opinion.

The Nonstop Talker. Listen for remarks which you can steer around to your objectives. Show him how your mission fits into his way of thinking. Be courteous and brief.

The Critic Crapehanger. Listen to his woes. Get all of his views. Give him some sympathy. Show an interest in him and his problems, and he may respond.

The Man in a Hurry. Be ready with pointed and important questions—questions he recognizes as meaningful. Phrase your questions in his language. Then he can see their importance immediately. Don't, under any circumstances, force him to guess. Put across your big questions early. It's the only way you can be sure you'll get to ask them at all.

Chip-on-his-shoulder. He thinks that if he opens his mouth he will put his foot in it—with your help. Chip away at his fears to show him that you are capable and impartial and that you need his help. You must sell yourself to him to get any response. Knowing the basis for his hostility gives you a chance to either skirt it or meet it positively. Find a hole in his armor.

Every man has a soft spot; your best bet is to find it.

How to Sidestep Arguments

No matter how wrong a person is, he can usually convince himself that he is right. He "loses face" if he has to admit that he is wrong. So, even though your blood pressure may shoot up at an interviewee's remark, you must not argue. Listen to the words of wisdom of Jonathan Swift: "Argument is the worst sort of conversation." Uncontrolled anger, which often comes from an argument, causes people to say things they do not mean. You may have strong convictions, but you can't toss them into conversational fires.

There are times, of course, when it is necessary to correct people. Even then, do it the tactful way. How can you side-step arguments? Here are some word tricks:

"You know I had exactly that same idea for years, but the other night I ran across an article by Dr. Garfinkel which stated that . . . ."

"Anybody might have made the same error . . . ."

"That is an interesting point of view. It never occurred to me before. You may be right, but I have always thought that . . . ."

"It is natural to suppose that happened in that way . . . ."

"I see your point, but how about this . . . ."

"Anybody might have gotten the same impression . . . ."

If you wish to avoid emotional fisticuffs, pay particular attention to people who get along with others and copy their strategies. Furthermore, promise yourself that you are going to drop habits which rub people the wrong way. If an argument is approaching, try discussion instead.

Help the other fellow to be right!

Sizing Up the Interviewee

When you want to influence people, you must be able to size them up. In doing so, it is important to remember that motives and attitudes are usually more meaningful than complexion or color of the hair.

You must observe each person's "peculiar magic," to use the words of Gerold Frank. Discussing the personality sketch in *Writer's Digest,* he summed up the bits of tell-tale evidence in this way: "However you define it, I think we'll agree that personality is made up of subtle things—a sense of humor, or a sadness or warmth; kindliness or harshness; a tartness of manner; a way of nodding one's head; the crinkles that form about one's eyes as one smiles—whatever it is that makes man what he is."

Pay special attention to the interviewee's voice, particularly to changes in inflection. Think for a moment of all the many meanings of the word *No.* When a person is excited, his voice usually rises. Psychologist Robert S. Woodworth assures us that "the voice is perhaps more expressive than the face." First note the words, with their associated meanings, then add the vocal tones and inflections, and the emotional expression becomes clear and finely shaded.

Watch for these clues to character and action:

(1) Note the primary qualities—the basic drives which make the person click.

(2) Think in terms of the other person—his ideas and prejudices (keep your prejudices out of it).

(3) Pay particular attention to details—specific and unique characteristics—which make the person different.

(4) Know all you can about the past behavior of

the person. Thus you can predict with some certainty what he may do, how he will react in the interview.

(5) Guard against forming a judgment the first time you see the person. Make your sizing up continuous through several situations.

Go in loaded and shoot for an angle.

Relaxation for Two

Your interviewee may face the experience of being questioned with some degree of anxiety. For one thing, he may be ill at ease in the presence of a stranger; indeed, he may cover his uncertainty by an appearance of arrogance or even anger. Or he may feel that the reporter is intruding into his personal affairs. And he may say, at least to himself, "This is my personal affair and I don't want anyone butting in on me." Help him to relax by using an indirect, easy-going, pleasant approach.

On the other hand, as a reporter, you may feel a certain inadequacy as you face the situation. Worries may pop into your mind. How can I break the ice? Will I say the right thing? What if he doesn't like me? Am I really competent to handle the situation? As John Darley reminds us in *The Interviewee in Counseling*, the interviewer may be a "bit frightened by the curtain's going up on a play in which he has not rehearsed his part." Careful preparation should give you a certain amount of confidence. Then, once the interview is underway, use all possible alertness, ingenuity, and personality to break down barriers.

To achieve the goal of becoming an expert interviewer, you must fortify your good traits and cut down on the use of negative ideas and approaches. You can avoid this emotional block by heeding Shakespeare's warning: "Our doubts are traitors, / And make us lose the good we oft might win / By fearing to attempt."

59

Learn to relax. A rubber band lasts longer if it isn't stretched too tight.

Persistence Pays Off!

Are you a Casper Milquetoast? Then you are eager to know how to get the drive, the resourcefulness, and the poise which are "musts" in obtaining information. Do some of your sources ask you to keep news out of the paper? When your immediate source fails, do you have other ways of getting the information?

Know what you want and then go after it. H. L. Mencken used this method when he wanted to get into the newspaper business. He asked Max Ways, city editor of the *Baltimore Morning Herald,* for a job. Ways turned him down and said he might call at some vague future time. Mencken went back the next day and was waved away. "The third night," says Mencken, "Max simply shook his head, and so on the fourth, fifth, sixth, and seventh." On the eighth—"or maybe it was the ninth or tenth"—Mencken was told to come back, only to be turned away again, and thus "it went on for four weeks, night in and day out." At last came the great day and Mencken's persistence was rewarded: Max Ways gave him his chance.

What is the difference between the expert reporter and the mediocre one? It is one word, "attitude." If your attitude is right, if nothing swerves you from your course, you can move up rapidly into the experts' class.

Don't give up too soon. Tactful persistence pays.

Hearing Is Not Believing

Can you "see through" statements of other persons? Philip Gibbs, special correspondent for the *London Chronicle,* did when he revealed Dr. Cook's fraud in claiming the discovery of the North Pole. First of all, Gibbs was twenty-four hours behind other correspondents when he got on the story. When he reached Copenhagen, the vessel bringing Dr. Cook had not arrived because of dense fog. Through a chance meeting in a restaurant with Mrs. Rasmussen, wife of the explorer, Gibbs got to Elsinore and aboard a launch which was putting out to meet the delayed ship. He was the only English-speaking person present at the first interview on shipboard.

Cook's eye evaded Gibbs' as he explained that he had no papers to prove his claim, not even a diary. When pressed for some sort of written record or notes, he exclaimed, "You believed Nansen and Amundsen and Sverdrup. They had only their story to tell. Why don't you believe me?"

Gibbs wrote a seven-column story in which he expressed his doubts and rushed it to the *Chronicle*. As a result, he was denounced and his life threatened. But not long afterward Gibbs' intuition paid dividends, and his story was recognized as one of the most notable scoops in the history of journalism.

Judge with your eyes open and your brain clear; then stick to your guns.

Some informants will try to fool you. On occasions, you may be "taken in." Here is Mr. Wallstreet, who must justify his decision, but he omits some of the facts. Or there is Mr. Distortion, who twists some facts to his advantage. And then there is the person who makes an honest mistake in his comments to a reporter.

Some of your interviewees may resort to "half-truths." As an interviewer, you must distinguish between lies due to mental conflict, lies of revenge, accidental lies, lies of vanity, lies as defense mechanisms, white lies, lies of loyalty, seeming lies which arise in differences in viewpoint regarding matters, and lies due to a desire to control the situation. "Most persons feel reluctant to tell a lie in so many words, but few have any compunctions in deceiving by manner, and the like, persons toward whom they have no obligation," declared Charles H. Cooley in *Human Nature and the Social Order*.

Getting the truth is sometimes tiring and discouraging, but that is your task as a reporter. How can you detect false statements? How can you see behind the cloud which obscures the truth? Here are a few suggestions:

First, know as much as or more about the subject than the interviewee. Remember you can't be too suspicious. Don't operate on the theory that everyone is trying to fool you, but be ready to take statements with a grain of salt.

Has this particular person ever fooled you before? Does he have a reputation for truthfulness and honesty? Show that you have confidence in him, and he may hesitate to fool you. Get his side of the story and indicate that you understand his position—his predicament. When he has "told all," he may listen to your suggestions. And remember that the other person always has a reason for saying what he does.

Is there a motive behind his statements? Does he have an axe to grind? Do his statements and opinions synchronize with the over-all situation? If not, why not? Does he "play dumb" just to throw you off the track? Be ready to check other persons and other sources for verification.

When in doubt, test for truth.

Get the "Inside Story"

Just how much interpretation a reporter can get into his story is always a problem. The scientific historian gathers his material, weighs the evidence, and selects what he believes to be the facts. Then he attempts to put those facts together in their proper order and against the proper background so that some perspective emerges. As the last step, he writes his story in such a way as to make his own findings clear to the reader.

This is the ideal situation. But most of the time the reporter cannot follow the pattern. Instead, he must spring into action, check his sources as quickly as possible, and then write his story. "The newspaper reporter must catch the train of history as it flashes by on the inside track," Donald Grant of the *Des Moines Register* says. He must write about individual events as they occur. Thus he cannot have the same detachment as the scientific historian. Above all, he must sense the news value of a situation and then fit it into the patterns of current history.

Mere quotations are never enough. You must show what the interviewee's beliefs or predictions will mean in the future. No reporter can afford to violate the dictum of Charles A. Dana that "the invariable law of the newspaper is to be interesting." As a good reporter, you will get a thrill out of seeing history as it is made.

Most news is a fragmentary thing. Every reporter starts with the facts and then he goes on to show what those facts mean. "And the meaning of the facts," W. M. Kiplinger says, "is much more important, illuminating, and digestible than the facts themselves."

What yardstick of news values can you use? Here are some to keep in mind: prominence, human interest, consequence, timeliness, proximity, personal appeal, and unusualness.

Remember: Readers like the "inside dope." So . . . watch for the news behind the news.

Make His Dreams Come True

Never forget that an appeal to your interviewee's desires is a powerful key to persuasion. Mr. J. Uppington

Gearshift may act and dress like the big tycoon he is, but he wants praise, prestige, advancement, and peace of mind. He wants to be understood—he wants to be appreciated. If the news story which comes from the interview brings Mr. Gearshift any of these things, he is bound to be interested. So sometimes you can say, "The public will get a better understanding of your point of view when the article appears."

On the other hand, sometimes you will find it an effective strategy to appeal to fear as well as to desire. A businessman, for instance, may have a greater fear of loss than the desire for profit. In this situation you may say, "If nothing is said, if nothing is published, people may wonder about the true conditions." Show him how the publication of the story will dissolve his fears.

In building your tentative techniques for an interview, take plenty of time to consider the basic desires and fears. Which of these desires can a news story help answer? What fears can you raise in the interviewee's mind that a published story might relieve? A word of caution: Use the fear psychology only when conditions warrant it.

Your best tool is the interviewee's imagination.
Use it to show him his dreams can come true.

Try a Little Tenderness

Many laymen seem to have the idea that reporters are hard-boiled and gruff. This is seldom so. Big reporters—successful reporters—are noted for their courtesy and consideration of others. Of course, when the occasion demands, a reporter can be rough and tough, but he doesn't have to act that way very often. Most of the time he can resort to more subtly persuasive techniques, techniques which are based on the Golden Rule.

When Dr. Norman Vincent Peale was a young reporter, he had to gouge news out of a rough-and-tumble police sergeant. "It was like bearding a lion in his den to talk with him," says Dr. Peale. "I found he had a little granddaughter, however, and soon realized she was his weakness. One night I surprised him by saying, 'How is that nice little granddaughter of yours?' He melted like snow in the springtime and became a fast friend."

Kindness works wonders. Kindness and sympathy are "musts" when you interview certain types of informants. You must be gentle and understanding when you are talking with elderly people, foreigners, small children, or anyone who is facing tragedy, fear, or sorrow.

Here's a special reminder: Avoid any strong persuasive strategy in talking to a person who is maladjusted, under great emotional stress, or mentally ill. Avoid "suggestion" in any form, psychologists advise. Avoid all suggestive influences, such as tone of voice and facial expression, which might determine the interviewee's associations.

Approach all of these persons in perfect candor. Let each know that you are Joe Smith, a reporter for the *News Record,* and that you have come for a certain story. Be patient. Help him all you can. Show an interest in him and his situation. Be understanding. Set out to win his confidence. The best way is to deserve it.

Kid gloves win more interviews than boxing gloves.

Develop Your Trustworthiness

Sometimes, particularly when you are dealing with a very shy person, you will have to build up his trust in you. Some people are shy by nature. Others shy from reporters—all reporters. By your total impact—personality, manners, attitude, voice, and know-how—you must convince such persons that you are competent and trustworthy.

Colonel Charles Lindbergh, an unknown mail pilot who flew the Atlantic and gained glory and fame, developed an acute dislike for all reporters because of the tremendous publicity which he received.

Lauren D. Lyman, aviation editor of the *New York Times*, found Lindbergh an extremely difficult person with whom to deal. But the newsman never allowed that fact to deter him from fair, objective reporting. Gradually Lindbergh learned that Mr. Lyman could be trusted. And years later, when Lindbergh decided to take his family abroad and wanted to be sure the story would not break until they were far out at sea, it was to Mr. Lyman that he confided it. The result? Lyman received the Pulitzer Prize for his scoop.

How can you build up the other fellow's trust in you? Arguing usually gets you nowhere. Attempting to "drive home" your points only arouses antagonisms. Rather, you must convince the other person that you can write an accurate, complete, and impartial story. You must demonstrate that you can handle the situation in a professional manner. Develop a reputation for integrity. Resolve to do your best in every assignment and then people will know that you are trustworthy.

You can climb higher when you travel on the level.

Be a Good Listener "First"

It is hard to keep your feelings and your views in the background as you contact persons for news, and it is just as hard to remain impersonal in your reactions.

Sinclair Lewis couldn't keep the lid on his feelings when he talked to people he did not like. Once he told a group at a press conference about being fired from a paper in Waterloo, Iowa, one in San Francisco, and the Associated Press. He grinned and asked, "Why? I was just naturally incompetent. If I liked the man I happened to interview, I'd go back and write a dandy story. If I didn't like him, my story would be a flop. How my wife [Dorothy Thompson] can remain interested in all the persons she has to talk to, I can't see!"

Only geniuses can afford to make enemies!

If you talk too much, you lessen the interest of the interviewee, take his valuable time, and may alienate him. Keep a curb on your own opinions, forecasts, peeves, and affairs.

Listen to people tell you about their exploits, their "big moments," and stay quiet about yours. Avoid putting in your "ten cents' worth" to let others know how almighty you are. Let others be the heroes—you can cheer them on.

Be a good listener first and a good talker second.

Check These Pointers to Step Up Your
Effectiveness in Interviewing.

Some "little things" may seem unimportant to you in your interviewing experiences but they can have a tremendous effect on your effectiveness. There are many of them. No one could list all of them, but they are important. Check your performance with the list on the following pages.

You will

always identify yourself to the interviewee

be on time if you have an appointment

be direct and confident in your techniques

be courteous even when friction develops

be interested in the interviewee and his subject

always know in advance what facts you are seeking

act interested even if the respondent gets off the subject

be sincere

use conversational "hooks" to keep the interview proceeding properly

make a positive impression

keep the interview informal

refrain from lecturing to the interviewee

respect the respondent's time

allow the interviewee to tell his story in his own way

be accurate

verify doubtful statements after the interview

watch for idiosyncrasies and traits which make the person unique

be at ease with the interviewee, thus helping him to be at ease

be on the alert for unusual angles, unexpected slants, and new facts

use correct English

keep the interview moving by the right kind of conversation rather than sticking to the question-and-answer method

68

THE INTERVIEWEE

You won't

      try to get in to see someone under false pretenses

      promise to print the remarks word for word

      take every statement at face value

      give up if the person doesn't know

      be afraid to ask what you want to know

      expect the interviewee to know the type of material you need

      misquote your source

      let the interviewee dominate the situation

      give advice or moral admonition

      drag out the interview beyond a reasonable point

      whistle, hum softly, or use your pencil to tap out your imitation of Gene Krupa while your interviewee is talking

      be offensive in your actions or words

      rush the interviewee

      forget the policy of your paper

      insult the intelligence of the respondent

      engage in gossip or petty conversation

      be thrown off guard by a sudden twist in the situation

      use stereotyped questions

      make threats except as a last resort in special cases

      act annoyed at interruptions

      distract the interviewee's attention with your mannerisms

You will

send the interviewee a list of questions beforehand
if the interview is to be a major one

listen attentively

show the interviewee that you know enough about
the subject to write the story accurately

make your questions clear

pronounce the name of the respondent correctly
and use it from time to time during the interview

obtain all the facts needed for a well-rounded story

express your thanks to the respondent at the close
of the interview

write the story while the information is fresh

How to Make Memories Stick

Two newsmen, John Kieran and Franklin P. Adams,
are known to millions for their memory feats on "Information Please." We are told that Beethoven could memorize a
complex musical composition by hearing it once or twice,
and that both Caesar and Napoleon knew thousands of their
soldiers by name. Lord Macaulay knew both Homer's *Iliad*
and Milton's *Paradise Lost* by heart.

As a reporter you need a good memory, too. Why?
Primarily, you need it in taking notes speedily and accurately. Then, you must associate comments and facts you obtain from the interviewee with past events, for you interpret

THE INTERVIEWEE

You won't

> forget when to leave
>
> acknowledge information with "Okey doke" or other objectionable expressions
>
> return to your typewriter and then think of important questions you should have asked.

current information in the light of all that has gone before. In addition, you must use your memory to recall what your interviewee considers important. He will be pleased that you consider something about him worth remembering. For instance, you greet Mr. Walltex cordially and then ask, "How is your golf game?" He beams and tells you. Then it is easy for you to swing right into the interview. How did you know to ask the question on golf? You jotted it down when you left him at a previous meeting, returned it to your memory, and pulled it out when it was needed.

The great secret in remembering is to associate the idea with the person. The more unusual or out of the ordinary the idea, the longer you remember it. Form a mental picture of Mr. Walltex playing golf. Jot down these words, "golf, Walltex." Sink them into your memory. Then when you see him again, he is highly flattered that you remembered his interest. Once you've given yourself an incentive to remember, you have already improved your memory.

A pad and pencil make you a memory expert.

You're Part Actor

Your success as an interviewer, like that of the actor, depends partly on your repertoire. You need a variety of strategies and attention-holders because your "audiences" change. On occasions, you must be part actor. You must adapt your mood, your actions, and your point of view to those of the interviewee. In the words of Richard M. Hunt, you cannot be a "machine with a pre-fabricated list of questions, but a living human being who listens, reacts, and moves freely along the lines of the subject's thinking."

At times, you must listen patiently when your subject gets off the track. When this happens, don't quit taking notes. That might offend him. It is best to scribble something —just anything—meanwhile thinking of your next question or of a polite way to get him back on the main subject. Avoid giving yourself away by looking bored.

You must guard against an overeagerness to say, "Yes, I understand," when your respondent has told you something. Such a reply may mean that you want to understand or that you understand in general. You may say this when you really mean to say, "Actually, I don't get you at all in your explanation of the operation of the electric computers in the newest fighter planes, so let's just forget that and go on to something which I can understand."

Also, when you answer "I understand" too readily, you may confuse and block the interviewee in his attempt to give the details which you need to write a sound story.

Just to be sure that you are getting all of the facts and details in their right relationship, you can make a statement of this sort: "Now I believe that I understand what you mean, but just to be sure I'll appreciate your running over the facts briefly once more." In this way, you have convinced the respondent that you seek both accuracy and understanding.

No reporter worth his salt will be overeager or overawed during an interview. The value of remaining calm and objective was pointed up by Jack Hamilton: "Don't go overboard in taking at face-value everything the interviewee may tell you. He may be talking to give a big impression to the boys in the backroom who know him well and will read his story. Weigh everything carefully, and counter-check."

World-shaking quotations don't come very often today from important persons. In fact, Mr. V.I.P. is not likely to say anything in an interview that he would not say in a public speech. Yet this fact should not keep you from making the most of an interview in sizing up the person. Anne O'Hare McCormick, who won the Pulitzer Prize for distinguished foreign correspondence in 1937, says that the person "does reveal himself, and this is of utmost importance to the interpretation of the action in which his character, his vanities and ambitions, his personal reactions, are decisive factors." Be alert, and if the desired information is not secured, then switch to writing a personality sketch. Watch for drama even in a dull situation.

No actor likes to play an empty house. Be a good audience.

How Hunches Spark Ideas

Sometimes you will know from your news sense that everything is just right for a person to talk. Because you are close to people, you know that they want the answer to a certain question. There is only one person who has that answer. So you go after him.

Keys to Successful Interviewing

Roy W. Howard, chairman of the board of the Scripps-Howard Newspapers, felt an urge of this sort to interview Stalin to discover the answer to the question being debated all over the world: "Is Russia going to war with Japan? If so, when and at what point will the break come?" The time was March, 1936. Stalin had not been interviewed since H. G. Wells' talk with him on July 23, 1934. Howard wired Stalin from Paris stating that he would be in Moscow on a certain date and requesting an interview for publication. When he arrived at the American embassy, he found a message granting an appointment. Conducted through an interpreter, the interview lasted for three and one-half hours. Howard's news sense and strategy clicked. His story was translated into some twenty different languages and dialects. As W. W. Hawkins, general manager of Scripps-Howard Newspapers, explained, "It was given to all who asked for it. . . . we considered it a public document—too big to be exclusive." Howard's news hunch worked.

Strange? No, not at all. But the thing to remember here is that the ability to "feel" the situation is the key. It will happen to you sooner or later. Your restlessness spurs you on; you contact the right person and he tells all. You get a rattling good yarn, good because your imagination sparked an idea.

Logic has its limits, so play your hunches.

Fundamentals Come First

By now you have seen some of the main strategies which the expert interviewer uses. You have seen that luck doesn't count particularly, nor does the occasion. Rather, there is a pattern, a flexible pattern which is followed by the top-flight writers.

Yet there is something beneath the pattern. It can be called "savvy" or "know-how." It consists of the basic qualities which every successful interviewer possesses. Here are some of the main ones:

Mental alertness
Courage
Punctuality
Patience
Ease in talking
Curiosity
Adaptability
Pleasing personal appearance
Endurance
Reliability
Drive
Optimism
Shrewdness
Sense of humor
Ability to control the situation
A news sense
Ability to deal with many types of personalities
Respect for the attitude of the interviewee (particularly one of another race, culture, social class, or economic level)
Sympathetic insight into the views and motives of the interviewee.

In the final analysis, remember that the best interviewing is the result of the battery of skills and abilities which the interviewer uses. His knowledge, his understanding, his sensitivity, his expertness in knowing human behavior—these are keys which open up the other person. And always, the expert interviewer knows that motivation is the moving force in the interaction of person with person.

Obviously, the traits exhibited by the interviewer are determined by the specific situation. He must have facility in dealing with people. Remember, too, that the reporter's own emotional balance must be so steady that irritation, disappointment, and failure have no power to alter his poise. He is adjusted to life. He isn't "thrown" by people and situations. He possesses what Adolf Meyer calls "constructive composure."

Somehow or other, you've got to get the "feel" of the situation. You won't get it by telephone. Meyer Berger of the *New York Times* writes his own stories without the aid of the rewrite desk. Why? He says, "A good story doesn't take on dimension until you see it. I always try to get life and sound and motion . . . and the only way you can do it is by being there."

Some Little "Secrets"

You will step up your interviewing skills much faster by following a few simple suggestions. They are easy to remember. They are easy to use. And they work magically.

First, what is the one trait that makes each interview an adventure? That word is "attitude." Look in the dictionary and you will find that the word means "the way you think, act, and feel." If you can think, act, and feel in tune with the other person, then you are sure to get results. Try your hardest to become interested in each person—even a bore—as an individual. Then notice the difference in his reaction. He will see your interest. He will feel it. And your assignment will be more resultful.

Secondly, if you want the other person to like you instantly, let him feel that you are favorably impressed with him. Be a good listener and enjoy it.

"I like to talk to people," Hal Boyle, Associated Press correspondent, declares. For the most part, he prefers to talk with people who make up the great masses of humanity. "Ordinarily," he says, "they haven't accumulated a crust of sophistication." Boyle finds great interest in talking with children, mainly because of their attitudes and vocabularies. He tells of the little girl who spent several hours looking at the dinosaurs, stuffed bears, and other exhibits in a museum. Upon being asked where she had been, she replied, "To a dead zoo."

Be alive to others. Develop "you-ability." Get the other fellow's angle. If you want to sell yourself, develop a genuine and sincere interest in others.

People are your business. Don't sell them short.

Practice These Suggestions

Always state the problem to yourself before the interview. Define your aims. Seek out points of individuality. What are you trying to do? What would the readers like to know? What do I want the interviewee to do? Ask these questions early and then plan your approaches.

Learn by doing and learn by observation. Watch all types of interviewers in action. Pay close attention the next time an insurance man calls on you. What techniques did Junior's teacher use when she dropped by your home on her visit the other night? Notice the strategies used by the credit manager the next time you establish an account. Watch the interviewing techniques used by your physician when you visit him for your annual check-up.

In each instance, analyze the interviewing process afterwards. Ask yourself these questions: What were the attitudes and conduct of the interviewer? Was he free from prejudices? Was he tolerant? Understanding? Helpful? Did he sense the special facts of my case? Did I feel at ease during the entire interview? Do I feel that the results satisfied both of us?

And you can add to your professional know-how by gazing at the vignettes of life about you. A successful writer who has rare competence as an interviewer told me, "I delight in watching persons in all sorts of interviewing situations. Many of them are informal—mostly small talk—but when the evidence is sifted, I have gained new knowledge for my use as a writer. The filling-station attendant giving directions to the tourist, the housewife asking the grocer about the new soap flakes, the moppet asking the ticket seller about the forthcoming cowboy movie—all these incidents and more through twenty years have given me invaluable information on behavior."

After everything else has been considered, isn't it imagination and a feeling for people which separate the mediocre interviewer from the master? You will agree that the only way to acquire that feeling is to live with people—people who keep the wheels of society moving, people who eat hot dogs, people who elect the president, mankind all about you.

> You must analyze each situation beforehand, strengthen your skills by action and observation, and study each situation immediately afterwards in terms of improved performance.

Here Are the High Points

Summing up this long chapter—long because it is important, and important enough to be read several times to get every tested technique, I would say:

> First impressions? Make yours positive.
> Use a planned approach, not a canned approach.
> Don't be so clever that you outsmart yourself.
> Watch your words and your words will work for you.
> Real appreciation comes from the heart—not from the lips.
> Bend over backward to understand, and the interviewee will usually go forward with you.

Do all you can to help the interviewee, not to confuse him.

If you are tempted to use pressure, use a new angle instead.

Keep your sense of humor, even when the going gets rough.

Remember that he who laughs, lasts.

Give the interviewee the center of the stage; you can give cues from the wings.

Keep this basic idea in mind: Offer your interviewee something which will help him—something which brings him closer to his heart's desire.

5
The Situation Sets the Pattern

TAKE A LOOK tonight through your favorite magazine or newspaper. Make your own count to discover how many of the interview stories are really more than "business as usual" treatments? How many read as though the writer saw a plus element in a routine situation? How many of the stories actually lure and hold you? How many sound as though the writer had telephoned someone, asked a few questions, and then thrown a few words together?

Now pick out an interview story that clicks. What gives it strength and pull? Select the factors—preparation, knowledge of human nature, skill in questioning, sureness of news values, good judgment, color and accuracy in writing, and dramatic quality—which make it ring. Now try to find the intangibles—objectivity, persistence, ability to find new angles, and others—which contribute to the story. Could you give a one-word summary of your findings? Yes, there is one word, an important word: *organization*.

Before a successful interview is completed, you must have a story pattern charted. Where does this pattern come from? From your savvy, your know-how, your imagination. Yes, and from your experience—the times when your interviews didn't click and you threw your mental gears in reverse and found out why. You have learned to be sensitive to little things—the many little things that give your stories sparkle.

The Situation Sets the Pattern

When you first write interview stories, you will consider the type of each one, and you will have a healthy respect for facts, opinions, timing, and news values. You will keep your eye on the main guideposts. Later you will do the right things by habit most of the time. Don't, however, feel bound by types and patterns if you strike an idea rich in news value and human interest. Make the most of the uniqueness of each assignment.

No interview can be any better than the story pattern which you hold before you. Without a plan which covers all principles, not just for rare occasions when celebrities come to town, but regularly, you cannot hope to increase your competency.

Do you feel that your interviews are mediocre, routine, or uninteresting? If so, you should probe deeply for the reasons and seek methods to remedy the situation. Here is one tip that usually enables any writer to improve his stories: Consider all possible angles and vantage points in a situation and then concentrate on the most unusual. This simple trick will generally lift your interviews out of the rut of sameness and make them interesting and exciting. And you will get a new thrill in turning out a variety of types of interview stories.

You won't learn the art of interviewing by merely having an idea, nor can you improve your techniques by remote control. You will learn by doing. You will pick up the skills of the experts. You will study all of the better-known types of stories for structure ideas and angles. You will combine your interest in people with skill in questioning. Then you will read your completed story and ask, "What does it actually say? How forcibly and interestingly does it speak?" The big test is, "Did it click?" Not "What type is this?"

Some interviews will come your way as assignments from the desk. For a number of these you will have time to familiarize yourself with the person and his interests. For others you will be sent out in a hurry, and as you talk to the person briefly, you must make your own rules. On still other occasions, your results will be limited only by your nose for news, your imagination, your industriousness, and your knowledge. Whatever the occasion, make the most of each situation.

No rule will tell you precisely what type of story should result from any interview situation. That will depend upon the circumstances, the news interests, the personalities involved, and many other factors. Don't waste time worrying whether the forthcoming interview can be classified as one type or another. Rather, be sure that your approach and objectives are right—tailor-made for the specific situation—regardless of the category into which your story will fall. When you have become adept, you will do the right things by habit and by hunch.

Since interviewing ranges from a cub reporter's efforts in getting a few facts for a routine story to the rare skills and judgment of the experienced newsmen, it is difficult to classify interviews into exact types. One type, for instance, may combine facts, opinions, and the personality of the interviewee. Another may limit itself to opinions. Classification, therefore, must be made largely on the intention of the reporter or the nature of the assignment rather than on the form of his copy.

Because of the many labels used by newspapermen in classifying the various types of interviews, the categories which follow by no means exhaust the list. Rather, they are given to illustrate some of the principal kinds of interviews used by newspaper and magazine writers today.

Feature Interviews

Both in the newspaper profession and among readers the word "interview" is often misused. While newsgathering by the reporter goes on continually and at least half of the news stories are obtained through the interview method, interviewing in the purest sense of the word is comparatively rare.

Writing the feature interview is an art. Edward Price Bell, famous for his excellent interviews, spoke with accuracy when he said, "First-rate interviewers may be likened to first-rate portrait painters, the one reproducing emotional and intellectual, the other physical, lineaments." He used another apt metaphor when he characterized the feature interview as a mirror held up to a remarkable personality.

Joseph Pulitzer's standard for interviewing is still sound. He preached to his staff that the interview should reflect the personality of the person interviewed, describing his dress, mannerisms, and habits.

Emil Ludwig, famous for his reporting, believes that of all forms of journalism, the interview is perhaps the most polished and entertaining. Some of his views appeared in *Editor and Publisher:* "The French, with the advantage of an easy and at the same time precise language to help them, are past masters in the art of the interview. They are closely followed by the Americans and Hungarians, who can boast of many masterpieces in this field. The Americans succeed through ingeniousness, the Hungarians through cunning. The fact that the ingeniousness may be affected and the cunning camouflaged, does not alter the truth that these two qualities, combined with talent and experience, are essential to real success in interviewing."

If you really want to give a portrait in words of a person, you must go behind the facts in *Who's Who.* Why did this man become a famous musician? Perhaps, like Irving Berlin, who leads all American song writers in endurance and output, he cannot read music or set his own paper. Was music second choice in his life? Maybe he wanted to become a doctor and drive the longest car in town. How did he get where he is? Is he aggressive and firm? Jovial? Critical? Even-tempered? Is he poised and sure of himself? What childhood incident might have affected his philosophy? Does his appearance fit his character? What does he do in his spare time? Does he have any strange quirks in his personality? What about his emotional cycles? Do enough wondering, and soon you will be putting the jig-saw pieces together into a personality portrait.

If you are writing a long biographical sketch, for example, you must do even more research, travel, and interviewing than you would in writing a short article. In the biography you face the task of reconciling and integrating all of the many and often contradictory facts of the subject's life. Knowledge of the person is not enough. Walter S. Campbell, author and teacher of professional writing, emphasizes that "the biographer must understand the man's background —the race, nation, country, and customs which shaped his subject."

Sometimes a casual remark by a friend will give you a key to the interviewee's personality. "Sure," someone will say, "Stanley was always fooling with electricity. Why, once he made an arc light and it blew out the neighborhood transformer. Then one day he and Mr. Ayer, the high school science teacher, worked out some kind of contraption so that the home economics girls could bake their cakes and pies for just the right length of time."

Growth of radio and television services, and of magazine publication has made it more difficult for newspaper reporters to obtain feature interviews. Persons who are catapulted into headlines—whether they are convicts or clergymen—are often offered large sums for their life stories, comments, or opinions by magazines, network officials, or syndicates. When this happens, the celebrity of the moment may hesitate to grant an interview to a newspaper reporter.

Your hero or heroine of the moment, no matter how rushed and in demand, can, however, hardly avoid granting some kind of interview to the press. If he is new in the public spotlight, his recently acquired press agent will usually arrange a meeting. Mr. Big's statements may not be very important, but they will be read with interest by those who slavishly watch his career. Words from his lips—no matter how trite and colorless they may be to you—will provide a vicarious release for those who are following the man of the moment.

Yesterday's "Mr. Somebody" is likely to be almost a nobody today. Any person who achieves distinction or notoriety through some achievement usually sooner or later finds himself mentioned, if at all, in smaller headlines. Fame always fades. The man who was worshiped as a public hero a few years ago may be found tomorrow in a musty basement room with his yellowed clippings. It is always news when a celebrity of yesterday stages a comeback. Singer Al Jolson, with the aid of two successful movies based on his life, did this in 1948. His case was exceptional.

Everyone loves to hear about dignitaries, heroes, celebrities, somebodies. Few readers are averse to reading of the doings of social leaders, millionaires, gangsters, athletes, and others featured in current headlines. You will talk to crackpots. You will interview world-saving evangelists. And you may come to the conclusion voiced by Robert Wilder of the *New York Sun* that "the world is peopled almost entirely by the half-mad and the charmingly irresponsible." Nevertheless, what the great and the near-great tell you will provide news, information, and entertainment for your readers.

Local Angles

Alert city editors watch national and state news developments which provide local angles. Suppose the state superintendent of public instruction announces in a wire story that the amount of money allocated to schools from the state treasury has been reduced for the coming school year. As a reporter, you call the city superintendent and the county superintendent and ask how the smaller appropriations will affect the city and county schools.

85

Watch trends or situations elsewhere, and perhaps you can localize an idea. Suppose another city reports an appreciable increase in the number of juvenile delinquents. "Is the same thing happening in Blankville?" would be the basic question for your interview.

Forecasts or Predictions

Experts in the Bureau of Business Research at the state university predict that the volume of business for the state should increase during the first three months of the year. Again, you can use a local slant. "Will the stores in our town share in this upturn?" would be your basic query in interviewing business leaders. In this type of story ·you answer the reader's question, "What's next?"

Surveys

Unlike the prediction story, which is built mainly on comments and observations, the survey type is usually based on facts or figures. News of food, for example, always ranks high in reader interest. So the reporter makes a survey of twenty stores regarding ten food items and compares the prices with those of a survey made six months ago. He also uses comments and opinions of a number of persons— retail grocers, wholesale grocers, and other persons allied with the food business.

Symposium or Concensus

Your city editor often suggests a concensus assignment, usually based on something in the news. "Go ask about a dozen people what they think of the water shortage," he directs. In preparing for this assignment, phrase your question so that you can use it on everybody. Then choose people in a variety of occupations for questioning—the housewife, the water superintendent, the kid on his way to the swimming pool, a taxi driver, a merchant, for example. The best topics for this type of story are those of a controversial nature which your readers are discussing.

For Facts

Since you cannot always be present when things happen, you must frequently obtain information secondhand from persons who were there or who are in a position to know what happened. And since eyewitness accounts are often contradictory, you should see as many persons as possible. Obtain the name, address, and identification of each person you question. Find out what part he played in the event. You will discover that many persons who have witnessed a crime or an accident are reluctant to give their names and addresses for fear of being summoned as witnesses in lawsuits. If they have given their names to a policeman, however, they will usually give them also to a reporter. In cases of this kind, you face another problem: Sometimes it is hard to find the people you wish to interview. Crowds disperse quickly.

Getting in touch with a person is often your biggest problem. People attend social functions, take vacations, and go on other trips without leaving word of their destinations. You must get on the trail. Check with your subject's friends. Call the places where he might be. Find and question his relatives. Genius in reporting, as in most other vocations, is simply the capacity to go after something and to stick with your search everlastingly.

From Mass Press Conferences

Not too many years ago the press conference was an honored institution. Modeled somewhat after the questioning period in the British House of Commons and conducted by newspapermen, it gave reporters an opportunity to question public figures to get their views on policies and decisions. But today the press conference has a different aspect. Newspapermen have charged that the continuity of questioning, the possibility of "off-the-record" remarks, and the whole atmosphere are being destroyed by movie cameras, microphones, television lights, the hurried movements of television engineers, radio technicians, photographers, the voices of both radio and television commentators, and the mass of wires and lines needed for klieg lights, flashbulbs, tape recorders, and live broadcasts.

The mass interview with the press, held more or less regularly by many public officials, is an old Washington custom. In no other world capital is it possible for correspondents to discuss policies so freely with the nation's executives. Theodore Roosevelt started first-hand presidential relations with the press. He was the first president to set aside a room at the White House for reporters. President Howard Taft attempted weekly conferences with the press, but he caused resentment by apparently favoring the correspondent of his brother's newspaper. Woodrow Wilson originated the semi-weekly mass interviews at the White House.

When these interviews are reported, the President cannot be quoted directly, without permission. Furthermore, the background material he supplies cannot be attributed to him in any form. His statements must be paraphrased. Any accredited correspondent or reporter may attend any of these conferences, regardless of the political policy of the newspaper which he represents. Any reporter can ask any question he chooses—within the bounds of decency. Of course, the President can word his reply to suit himself. Sometimes he may give a detailed explanation; at other times he may evade a direct answer. On still other occasions he may resort to the "off-the-record" response that may tell the reporter much or little, but binds all present to secrecy. It hardly needs to be pointed out that any press conference with the President is important, though some are more news-worthy than others. At their best, such conferences set a key-note for other events.

Rarely ever does the President grant a private inter-view. Franklin D. Roosevelt gave a private interview to Arthur Krock, for which the latter won the Pulitzer Prize. At his next press conference the President apologized for granting the interview to the *New York Times'* correspond-ent in Washington.

Reporters should not and do not confine their cover-age of any type of news to press conferences. Almost every public official, whether serving as mayor of Middleberg or president of an industrial empire, is eager to get a "good press." If he is even mildly alert in his press relations, he will pass along the news and the reporter will go out of his way to give a "break" to his news source.

Many reporters dislike the mass press conference. As Paul R. Leach of the Washington Bureau of the Knight Newspapers told me, "I don't like 'em, but they've become a fixture in public life. My practice in mass interviews has been to let others ask the questions while I listen, noting questions or answers which need amplification or explana-tion, or perhaps a touch of color is lacking. I throw in my questions after the conference has progressed to the point where I want answers that I doubt I'm going to get other-wise. I might have specific questions in which only my papers would be interested. I reserve them for the time when the conference is slowing down. At a press conference I like to sit near two or three men I know will be asking interesting questions so that I can put in my nickel's worth when I see what they're driving at."

L. Lacey Reynolds, chief of the Washington bureau of the *Toledo Blade,* believes that the press conference should be distinguished from the interview. The former "can often-times become a trite and unproductive affair, in which many reporters seem to be more interested in trying to trip up the person being interviewed than in getting his point of view," he says.

About four-fifths of the questions asked at the White House press conferences are trite, Reynolds believes. Yet the one-fifth "has produced a great deal of news, over the years." Why so many trite questions? Reynolds has an answer to that: "Many of the trite questions are asked by people who want to tell their grandchildren that they once asked the President of the United States what it was all about. There is a certain amount of show-offness involved also."

At its best, the mass interview can give you a big story on which you can get an even break with other reporters, background for use in future stories, a tip which can be developed into a story which you dig up and write on your own, and an opportunity to see how the person reacts in the lively give-and-take which characterizes the mass interview.

Televised Press Conferences

Now that televised press conferences are being held, some reporters say that the intrusion of the new medium is coming close to wrecking the whole press-conference system. James "Scotty" Reston of the *New York Times* suggested after the National Republican Convention in 1952 that a detailed study be made of the whole problem to establish "ground rules." In *Editor and Publisher* he made the following suggestions: (1) There must be rigid control of who gets into the conference; (2) there must be an agreement that the subject being interviewed will not come within his partisan claque; (3) a way must be found to develop the "progressive" or follow-up question; and (4) reporters must discipline themselves to give others the opportunity to develop their lines of questioning.

Complaints about the bad effect of television coverage on the press conference are many. They fall into the following categories:

1. The "balance of power" shifted from the interviewer to the interviewee. As soon as an important question is asked, the subject is taken "off the hook" by a completely different question on another subject and evasive answers cannot be followed up.

2. The "showoff" tends to dominate the questioning, while the thoughtful, reflective reporter tends to sit back and not ask questions. Also, some conferences are so noisy that only those reporters in the front rows can hear.

3. Television men using amplifiers can dominate the questioning, while newspaper reporters must rely on their natural voices.

4. Newspaper reporters are being "turned for free" into actors for another medium.

5. Newspapermen do the "pick-and-shovel" work seven days a week, and untrained, largely inexperienced television men move in and capitalize on the big stories. Let them meet some of the responsibilities of the day-to-day original news coverage, say newspaper reporters.

6. The once frequently used transition from on-the-record to background information has disappeared. A person before a television camera cannot turn a switch and give reporters the benefit of his background information off the record, to be used but not attributed, as was the case in the "old days."

Mr. Reston is also worrying about another growing television practice. In Washington, he said, the situation has arisen where an official will withhold news from the press, make an arrangement for an appearance on one of the many television programs, and announce his news there, where he obtains more personal publicity and is not subject to serious questioning.

"The press conference is an instrument vital to democratic processes," Mr. Reston observes, "and it is being overwhelmed by paraphernalia."

Current big-time press conferences are sheer waste of time, effort, and nervous energy. That criticism was voiced by Walter T. Ridder, Washington correspondent of St. Paul and Duluth newspapers, in *The Quill*. He suggested that if press conferences are to have any value, they must be held separately from sessions with radio and television.

Many modern press conferences accomplish little, Ridder points out. Surveying the results, he says that reporters have never had an opportunity to throw anything more than hasty questions, the interviewee has had no opportunity to give thoughtful and considered answers, off-the-record or discoursive elucidations have been impossible, any fully rounded series of questions have likewise been impossible, and the whole affair has been conducted on such a catch-as-catch-can basis that little of a constructive nature has been accomplished.

What is the solution? Ridder suggests that newspaper and magazine writers hold their own press conferences, "free from the carnival-like atmosphere of present interrogations." This could be accomplished through organizations such as Washington's Overseas Writers, which strictly controls its membership list and the conditions under which speakers appear before the club. Ridder also suggests that only reporters with bona-fide credentials be admitted to press conferences. Unless something is done, he says, "the press conference will wither from lack of reporters."

Newsmen will do a better job because of televised interviews is the view of Joe Hainline, former NBC reporter in the Pacific and now newscaster at radio station WJR, Detroit. Writing in *The Quill*, he stated: "Good newspapermen will continue to participate in important press conferences so long as such conferences are held. They will learn to live with this modern medium of communications, or they will be left behind." He believes that those who are unable to compete will pass the way of "the buggy whip and the Stanley Steamer." But those who survive "will be more accurate and more objective in their reporting because they no longer enjoy a monopoly on the dissemination of news."

Success of a press conference depends to a great degree upon the co-operation of the respondent. If he is co-operative and not too thin skinned under the barrage of questions, he can make the meeting profitable to himself, to media representatives, and to the public. On the other hand, if he is reluctant to co-operate and is sensitive to press and radio criticism, the news conference suffers accordingly.

James E. Pollard, a recognized authority on the White House press conference, believes that it is here to stay. "After nearly four decades of continuous and expanding use," he observes, "it appears to be a fixture between the chief executive and the American people through the media of the press and the radio. It seems doubtful that any future president will find it possible or politic to hamstring it or to do away with it."

Interviews for Opinions

Policy statements. "What program have you planned for the year?" you ask the new president of the chamber of commerce as he takes office. What he plans to do is news, but it is bigger news if the course he plans to follow is different from that of former presidents. His plans make more exciting news if they possess elements which are controversial. This type of story is not confined to business and civic affairs. Interview the new pastor of the First Methodist Church soon after his arrival in your city. His statements may make the headlines.

Farewell stories. You get a tip this afternoon that the janitor at the courthouse will retire Friday. He has been on the job for twenty-eight years, so there's a story there. You can interview a person when he reaches the end of his term in office. Then there is the more exciting type of farewell story: public officials who resign or are discharged.

Their statements may contain revelations which can be played up in big headlines.

Refusals to comment. Sometimes a person grants you an interview and then refuses to talk. His silence may be more important news than any statement he could have made. List the questions which were asked so that readers can draw their own conclusions. Your story might describe your experiences in not getting any replies. Warning: If you could not reach the person, always say so in the story.

Announcements. Mr. J. Uppington Didgit, president of International Steel, Inc., calls or grants a press conference when he has something to say. To the reader, the story sounds like an announcement, but the material was probably obtained from the interviewee by steady questioning. Many public officials use this means of releasing facts, views, or predictions on topics which have strong news interest. They may give reporters a special release and also allow time for special questions.

Parting words. As athletes and coaches left the United States for the 1952 Olympic games in Helsinki, sports writers filed many stories on the parting words of American representatives. You can use the same question, "What do you have to say before leaving?" when a county delegation prepares to confer with members of the highway commission at the state capitol regarding new roads.

Follow-up. Follow-up stories lend themselves to a variety of interview situations. Ask the federal inspectors if they ever found any clues to the post-office theft nearly two years ago. Ask the dietician at Taft Junior High School if the new menus which she proposed last September improved the health of the children as she had hoped they would. Get a statement from the candidate who won—and from the candidates who lost, if they care to talk.

Quickies. You are likely to bump into a celebrity at the most unexpected moment. Tomorrow you may walk into your favorite coffeeshop and find the governor finishing his meal. Even if you are totally unprepared, you should be able to ask questions. He may not say much that is important, but the brief story will be read with interest. On most occasions publicists will inform your newspaper when their clients are to appear in your community—even though Mr. Big has just five minutes between planes. And even if the celebrity doesn't say much, he may be photogenic.

Birthdays. Just any birthday, even for someone who has gone beyond three-score and ten, isn't necessarily news. But if a person reaches the 100-year mark, then an interview will certainly yield bits of philosophy and advice. For one thing, you will find that the oldster delights in reminiscing about his past.

The average life expectancy in the United States is now sixty-seven years. And believe it or not, there are more than 12,000,000 people who are more than sixty-five years old. This vast public is probably the most ignored of all publics served by today's newspaper. Remember this public, first for news, photographs, and feature stories which will interest its members. Then determine that you are going to get more interviews from oldsters. Stories about them rank high in reader interest.

Handouts. Reporters may find tips and facts in "handouts" released by publicists. On occasion, when newsmen may be barred from a conference or a meeting, a press assistant may issue a release. He may brief reporters on certain aspects of the affair. Much of this material is accurate and newsworthy. Yet the facts are usually presented so that they make a favorable impression for the person, organization, or agency releasing them. The worth of the material is dependent upon many factors, including the reliability of the source, its motives, abilities of the writers, and so on. Since handouts are usually distributed to all correspondents, they are without the element of exclusiveness.

Handouts are sometimes released after actions are taken. The decisive point in many great events comes long before the event happens. Obviously, the top-flight reporter cannot place too much reliance on certain types of press releases. Often he can get an idea or angle from a handout and then start an investigation for a story of his own.

Blind interviews. You will find that most interviewees will allow use of their names with the facts, opinions, and comments which they have given you, but not always. Here is a high government official, for instance, who can give you newsworthy facts—and even allow the use of direct quotes—if his name is not connected with the story. As another example, you are asked to get a story from a mother whose teen-age son is a dope addict. You get the story—filled with quotations (warning parents and youths of the agony which comes with addiction)—and use it without mention of the mother's name because she has asked that it remain a secret. The alert and resourceful writer will find ways to indicate that what he reports is authoritative, even though he does not use names. The best-known examples of blind interviews are the scores of stories rushed from Washington, quoting "men high in official circles."

Denial stories. A denial story may spring from a published interview. It usually comes about in this way: A person quoted in an interview issues a denial of the statements attributed to him. He may even insist that he did not see the reporter. If the newsman is not guilty of misquotation, he may "stick to his guns" and write another story in which he asserts that his original account was correct, backed up, of course, by his newspaper.

Can denial stories be prevented? One way to pre-check, of course, is to show the write-up to the interviewee, but few newspapers favor such a practice. For one thing, the subject will probably delete everything the least bit unfavorable to him; for another, such a practice means delay. Most serious, when a story is submitted to the interviewee for approval, the newspaper's privilege to gather information and write stories as it deems best is surrendered.

The Situation Sets the Pattern

Production interview. You have read the excellent interviews published in *U. S. News and World Report,* which also attempts to cover both sides of questions by interviewing persons who hold opposite points of view. Although these interviews are unique in a sense, in reality they are a revival of an old technique.

The theory of the interview has always been accepted by American journalism, but journalists have not always followed through in presenting interviews in the best possible manner. The modern press conference permits such a wide variety of questions that frequently there is no coherence when it is reported. Likewise, reporters use "indirect discourse" to relate much of what is told them, with the result that the reader does not have an opportunity to judge for himself from the exact words of the principal of the interview.

In the case of *U. S. News and World Report,* the magazine had to decide that it would give substantial space to the interview—more than is possible in the usual newspaper. Actually, the technique employed is quite simple. The editors gather around the person being interviewed, and while they do not have any rehearsal in advance and usually do not have any prepared questions, the interview is carried on with as much co-ordination as possible. Each man waits for another to finish his questioning, whereas in a press conference there are frequent interruptions and the line of thought is often cut off before a conclusion is reached.

The mechanics of handling this type of interview are also quite simple. It is customary to submit the interview for correction and revision, so as to make sure that what is finally printed is actually authorized by the person interviewed. This means that usually an interval must elapse between the time of the interview and the time of publication, but this delay has proved helpful because it gives the person interviewed an opportunity to make sure exactly what he wants to say.

These interviews have attracted attention throughout the country. Readers of *U. S. News and World Report* have frequently stated that they get, as a result of the steady series of interviews, a vast amount of information which they feel comes first-hand to them, without any coloration or editing or paraphrasing of the ideas of the principal himself.

Miniatures. Editors of both metropolitan and small-town newspapers realize that a column of miniature interviews ranks high in reader interest. The reporter may ask several persons, "How did you earn your first dollar?" or he may quiz eight or ten persons on a current topic. Most editors brighten the column by using thumbnail pictures of the persons interviewed. Ordinarily the reporter states the question asked, where asked, and what time at the top of the column. Typical of these brief interviews are the "What Do You Think?" column in the *Oklahoma City Times* and the "Now You're Talking" column in the *Chicago Herald American.*

Summing up. What type of interview should you employ? Obviously, it will depend upon the nature of the assignment, the personality of the interviewee, the time, the news objectives, and all of the variables that make the experience unique. No rule can give you the exact answer. Most of the time you must use your own news judgment in making the most of the situation. Get the assignment straight in your mind and then it will be easier for you to guide the interview. Hit straight for the bull's-eye of reader interest. Squeeze all of the drama possible out of the situation. Get that in your story, and you can forget all about types.

6

It's How You Bait the Hook

YOU HAVE KNOWN REPORTERS like Bill. Mysteriously he inspires confidence in the other person—without any noticeable techniques—and soon the interviewee is talking. There are people to whom you unaccountably want to tell things. Bill is this type of man. F. H. Collier of the *St. Louis Globe Democrat* says that these persons are the natural-born reporters—"the confidants of the world."

How can you emulate Bill? How can you step up your effectiveness in the art of asking questions? To begin with, you can evaluate your present techniques. Discard the ones that don't produce results. Polish up the better ones. Observe the techniques of successful interviewers. Above all, do not say to yourself, "I'm just not the type—my personality is not adapted for that sort of thing." You can harness inner powers which will push you along the road to effective action. "Talent is our affair," said Gustave Flaubert. We can shrivel it through disuse, or we can build it up by creative exercise. We can keep on going through the same motions, or we can use our energy in acquiring skills of master interviewers.

Look forward to your next interviewing assignment as an adventure. Avoid the cut-and-dried way of formulating questions. Do a little "supposing." Picture the situation. Cast your mind hither and thither, forward and backward, in search of alternatives, in search of "what-if's" and "what-else's," and in search of new approaches. While using your imagination, be sure to jot down your ideas, because as Frank Bennett advises, ". . . like meteors, they are fleeting and soon gone if not jotted down."

If you are going to write an interview story that will get itself seen and read, you must first go out and establish a common meeting ground with your respondent. If you don't know that he is interested in Cuban farm products or bridge, you can hardly hope to catch his attention by starting in the middle of your subject.

Your starting point—the interest booster—must be found in the realm of something the interviewee already knows, from which you can logically lead to the basic reason for your meeting. By going halfway to meet your interviewee, by establishing a common ground, you win his confidence through your agreement on things in which he already believes. He is then predisposed to agree with you—if the right elements are present—on the matters into which your questions will carry him. Briefly then, your opening techniques must have arresting power. When these condition the interviewee properly, then it is easier for you to take him over into the realm you want to explore.

You must get in step with the other person. To do so, you must find out what makes him click, what he considers important—his goals in life. As has been emphasized before, you can obtain some clues by advance preparation. If time does not permit this step, you can ask questions during the interview. Listen carefully to his answers for clues to the direction to take in your interviewing techniques. "If there is any one secret to success," said Henry Ford, "it is in the ability to get the other person's point of view and see things from his angle as well as your own."

What advance preparation pays the biggest dividends? What "something more" will bring desired results from your questions? "Go in loaded!" says Dwight V. Swain, free-lance writer and instructor in professional writing in the University of Oklahoma. He makes ten concrete suggestions:

1. Know enough about your interviewee and his specialty to be able to talk intelligently.

2. Plan a tentative story in advance, so that he will either have to confirm or to contradict.

3. Stress a "what-how-why" approach. Leave the yes-or-no answers to the lawyers; you want explanations and details.

4. Match your questions and approach to your respondent's personality, rather than to his specialty. Learn to read his feelings—shyness, boredom, weariness, or anger—from his manner.

5. Don't be afraid to inject your own personality into an interview. Your man may be scared. Show him that you are friendly, human, and interested. Or figure out how he is feeling and then establish a common ground by letting him know that you have felt the same way at one time or another.

6. Never sit in judgment. Even sex killers resent contempt.

7. An interviewee will almost always try to help you if you admit frankly that you don't know anything about a subject, but a stupid question that shows unconscious ignorance frequently will freeze him.

8. Do hunt for questions that will start your respondent talking—even if on subjects unrelated to your interview.

9. Misquotation or misrepresentation of a man's position often breaks down flat refusals to talk.

10. Pretending to know more than you do encourages the fearful to give confirmation. But it's tricky—watch out, or you may get tripped up.

You have covered enough conventions and luncheon club meetings to know that many speakers get off to a slow start. Eventually some of them gather momentum and say something of interest. What is wrong? Each speaker lacks an attention-getting statement or gimmick in the first few words.

As an interviewer, you must capture and hold the attention of the person you are interviewing. Your approach may be so slow and ponderous that your interviewee loses interest before you begin. It can be so telegraphic—jumping right into the middle of your mission—that you never catch him at all; he doesn't know what you're talking about.

There are two types of attention: voluntary and involuntary. Your interviewee is bombarded by countless stimuli and countless attractions (even when the two of you are alone in his private office). First of all he attends to those things which he cannot avoid because they force themselves on him. That is involuntary attention. In the second place he gives attention to the things he wants to notice. That is voluntary attention. You may get the appointment for the interview by getting the person's attention involuntarily. Then you can rely on a variety of techniques when you have his voluntary attention. Caution: Always make your appeal relevant to the forthcoming interview. Any other appeal is questionable.

Psychologists remind us that the range of attention is limited. In the case of words, tests show that the average person can grasp the meaning of possibly five or six words at a glance. Remember, then, that the interviewee's attention fluctuates; hence it is wise to keep questions short or break up more involved queries.

Gear your questions to the chief interest of your subject. Remember that the person's likes, tastes, and wishes are projections of himself. The fisherman is not of the same cut and mind as the golfer. The musician has unique interests and is different from the minister. In reaching any of these people, the more you can approach them as individuals with individual tastes, ideas, and preferences, the better they will respond.

It's How You Bait the Hook

It is not enough for you to ask yourself, "Now just what would make me respond?" It is better to try to forget your own interests and decide what will make your interviewee talk. You must remember that he is more than Judge Smith, he is more than an officeholder, he is more than just another person who pays taxes and belongs to a lodge, he isn't just a statistic, he is a real person.

Your questions should be sincere. Sometimes you may have to promote that sincerity in yourself. If you know people—really know them—you will like them. Back of your sincerity, you must be sold on yourself, your job, and your calling. Unless you are sincere, the other person will never react, emote, or respond quite the way you want him to.

Never lead off with the big questions. That is the advice of Delbert Willis of the *Fort Worth Press:* "This may blow up the interview before it gets started. It will serve to cause the subject to throw up an immediate guard and tighten up like a clam. Get the conversation started first.

"Build into the big questions for a climax. After working up a sympathetic understanding, let the subject know that you *expect* him to answer the big questions. If he starts hedging, then is the time to argue your case. The information is going to come out anyway, maybe, so why not let you write the story. You understand his case. It is far better to let you write it than someone who has no appreciations of his plight."

To what extent are most persons talkative? Are there more extroverts than introverts? Little research has been done on the correlation between personality types and opinions. Jap Stapel, director of the Netherlands Institute of Public Opinion, asked interviewers for his organization to classify the respondents' personalities. In an article, "The Convivial Respondent," in *The Public Opinion Quarterly,* he reported that "We found a high consistency from survey to survey in the classifications made by interviewers. Between 56 and 62 per cent of all respondents were classified as 'easy-going, talkative, convivial' in the six surveys, while from 31 to 37 per cent were classified as 'reserved,' and between 8 and 12 per cent were unclassifiable." He cautions readers to remember, in accepting these results, that there is an element of vagueness in the qualities under consideration.

Questions of the right kind always win people. When Theodore Roosevelt was serving as president of the United States, he opened the White House doors to scientists, sportsmen, experts on literature, and other notables. Roosevelt's astonishing success in fascinating other men has often been misunderstood. Because his knowledge of men and events was versatile, many have thought that he charmed others by talking about his views and beliefs. Actually, just the opposite was true. He literally pumped men dry with questions. His secret? He thrilled the other fellow with his eagerness to learn.

By listening intently, you can charm the other person to a marked degree. More important, it is one of the most effective methods of inducing people to talk. In the days when William Randolph Hearst controlled a publishing empire, John K. Winkler said of him, ". . . for a man of large affairs and crowded appointments, [he] is the world's best listener. . . . When he . . . wishes to please, Hearst can be as winsome as a woman."

More reporters could use showmanship to a greater advantage. One of the basic principles of showmanship, for instance, is to demonstrate. Never take it for granted that the person will respond to mere words—show him. Suppose you are seeking some statements from a man you know to be reticent. Merely urging him to give his views won't work. Take along a copy of the morning paper and tell him, "Now here's what Senator Claghorn said in his speech last night. What is your answer?"

One imaginative reporter was asked to get the views of eight or ten leading citizens on the deplorable condition of the city's garbage dump. He made the rounds. No one said much. Then he decided to rent an automobile and ask the group to visit the dumping grounds. All of them responded. On their return they gave the reporter the statements he had been seeking. His strategy: he appealed to their basic sense of sight and smell.

Try it yourself. When a tough situation confronts you, seek an element of showmanship to get results. How can you do this? First, use your imagination and put yourself in the interviewee's place. Then—and this is the most difficult step—ask yourself what appeals would be dramatic and unusual enough to make you respond. Think of ways of presenting your case to the eye as well as the ear. Keep the spotlight on the interviewee. He is the leading character in the drama. Add a few bits of showmanship to your interviewing methods, and you will be gratified by the results.

Before giving your questions final approval, ask yourself, "Now just how much am I taking for granted?" Perhaps your respondent has only a hazy idea of the subject. He may confuse it with something else. It may be so vague to him that he has no means of forming judgments. And even though your interviewee may know the subject, he may misunderstand your question and give an unexpected answer.

Pollsters use several effective questioning techniques to make sure that their concepts are the same as those of the respondents. One method of avoiding misinformation is known as the "filter approach." To pin-point the area of information, the pollster may ask, "Have you ever heard of such-and-such?," followed by, "What examples can you give of such-and-such?" If the respondent knows little or nothing of the subject, then it may be necessary to make an explanation before asking further questions.

Perhaps you are thinking, "Why, it would be ridiculous for me to explain something to an interviewee." Not always. You have observed that different people will read directly opposite meanings into the same words. There is the whiskered story of the fellow who was asked by a friend,

"Is your wife entertaining this winter?" and answered, "Not very." Always define your subject, phrase your questions into words of everyday usage, and be sure that the interviewee's answers are in the frame of reference you intend.

What about the choice of words in questions? Simple words may not be enough to get the desired response from the man who sits in the easy chair with his thoughts elsewhere. Charles T. Estes, writing in *The Quarterly Journal of Speech*, points out that unless the receiver is on the same wave length, the character of what is sent out hardly governs the communication process.

Of course, it helps for the reporter to put what he has to say in clear, "listenable" language. He should do everything possible to define, simplify, amplify, and illustrate what he says. Such a procedure is all to the good, but, as Irving J. Lee reminds us in his book, *How to Talk with People*, "The listener has a job to do, too." Two persons must react to complete the communications process.

In addition, words do not always have the same meanings or connotations. Usage varies through the years. Years ago, when King James II observed that the new St. Paul's Cathedral was "amusing, awful, and artificial," he implied that Sir Christopher Wren's recent creation was pleasing, awe-inspiring, and skillfully designed. In short, what your interviewee understands from your words or statements may not be what you intended.

Be wary in using colloquialisms or provincialisms and similar forms of speech. In some sections of the nation "squaw candy" means salmon. Down in the cattle country of the Southwest "ridin' the grub line" refers to a cowboy's going from ranch to ranch accepting meals without paying for them. Like slang, the colloquialism seems more expressive than straight talk. For purposes of the interview, however, provincial or colloquial speech does not seem to have any great advantage, even when you are talking with habitual users. Furthermore, the degree of understanding among a particular group may be highly variable. Avoid being too "folksy."

You probably have seen the cartoon of the cub reporter—undoubtedly filled with pride to represent the press —trying to impress his first interviewee with these words, "Our sheet will be tight today, so let's get going so I can make the bulldog edition." Such newspaper slang isn't understood by most persons. Sometimes slang may make your questions more expressive, but be sure that it will be fully understood by the interviewee before you use it.

Your manner of phrasing questions is all important. Obviously, it is impossible to draw up a series of arbitrary rules for the phrasing of questions; nevertheless, any reporter can, through a study of the reactions to particular questions he has used, come to recognize principles, techniques, and phrase-making methods that are easier for interviewees to handle.

Interviewer-report forms used by field representatives of the National Opinion Research Center were examined in order to increase their efficiency. Paul B. Sheatsley, in a study of "Some Uses of Interviewer-Report Forms," which appeared in *The Public Opinion Quarterly*, reported that the following types of phrasing and construction of sentences make questions difficult to handle: (1) long questions, with several clauses or sentences; (2) unfamiliar words or concepts; (3) misplaced emphasis or no emphasis; (4) several ideas in the same question; (5) vague words or phrases, ambiguous antecedents, or personal pronouns; (6) irrelevant or repetitious words or phrases; (7) questions that lead to endless qualifying or that lack clear-cut categories; (8) abrupt shifts from one topic to another; (9) confused order of questions; (10) difficult question asked early in the interview; (11) identical questions repeated many times for different items; (12) open question calling for spontaneous articulation of ideas; and (13) questions that frequently draw answers in irrelevant terms (ends for means, hopes for expectations, what should be done instead of what is being done, and so on), rather than making explicit the proper terms of the reply.

It should be emphasized that factors contributing to the ease or difficulty of the newspaper interview are not exactly the same as those entering into interviews for polling groups. It is true, however, that a number of the same factors are present in both situations and that the reporter can profit from the National Opinion Research Center studies.

Questions fall into several categories. In one type the reporter phrases the words to suggest or prompt a specific answer. This is called a "leading question." In another type the newsman puts the question in general terms, without expecting a particular reply. In the latter case, you might ask, for instance, "What are your favorite television programs?" This is known as an "open question" or a "free-answer question" and and is so named because it is open to any answer.

Both kinds of questions may be desirable in a certain situation. If the interviewee is an elderly person, for instance, and has some difficulty in recalling names, then you may ask, "Wasn't it Francis Travers who was president of the church board at that time?" and the person says, "Yes, that's it!" On the other hand, if the person is confused or embarrassed, he may echo in his reply the words used in the question and so unwittingly fail to speak the truth. Although the leading question must be used with care, you will find that oftentimes a person cannot be pinned down to a proper answer except through its use.

Pollsters use other types of free-answer questions, Stanley L. Payne points out in *The Art of Asking Questions*. These include: (1) "opener" or introductory questions (they lead into the subject—provide background); (2) suggestions ("What could the schools do to improve teacher-student relations?"); (3) follow-up questions (for further elaboration); (4) reason-why ("Why do you say that?"); (5) argument type, usually in pairs ("In what ways would you say it is good?"; "In what ways could it be improved?"); (6) knowledge or memory tests ("As you recall it, what brought about this federal regulation?"); (7) source ("Where did you get your information?"); (8) probes ("Anything else?"; "Are there any others?"); and (9) precoding ("About how many people would you say live in the United States?"), in which logical groupings are set up beforehand.

Certainly the open or free-answer question has its advantages. For one thing, it imposes the necessity of thought on an interviewee. In relating facts or experiences, he will tell only what he remembers. Yet his response may through carelessness or oversight omit certain details. Indeed, he may withhold information that he considers irrelevant. In general, the open question provides a good introduction to the main subject and provides the background for other questions; furthermore, the reporter can use it to elicit reasons and to obtain additional material.

Hans Zeisel feels that an open question may yield unsatisfactory results because of the great amount of leeway it gives the respondent. But, he warns, in *Say It with Figures,* that in making the question more specific, the reporter must not force the respondent to form and express an opinion on a topic to which he has not previously given any thought.

Then there is the two-way question, which is at the other extreme from the free-answer type. It is sometimes called the "dichotomous" or the "bifurcated" type by social scientists and polling experts. As its name connotes, it is intended to suggest only two possible alternatives: yes or no, rich or poor, black or white, ill or healthy, left or right, this or that—choices that may be given to the interviewee.

Although this type of question suggests only two choices, it may produce an unexpected response. The interviewee may answer "I don't know," or he may not express an opinion at all. And although you may encourage him by saying, "Just give me some idea" or "Which way seems better?" he may still insist that he does not know.

Suppose you are quizzing the city manager. From what he has said you can't tell whether or not he plans to attend the highway conference in a neighboring city. You ask, "Are you going to Blankville or not?" He may give a qualified answer, such as, "Not if the weather stays cold," or "Yes, unless I decide to meet with the parks committee," or "Probably." In other words, there are times when you cannot get a positive answer, and in all truth the respondent may not know what he is going to do.

You can set the stage for stating a two-way question on an issue by making an introductory statement. For instance, you might say something like this: "Some legislators say that the names of all those receiving old age assistance should be published as a matter of record. Others say that such a published list would only embarrass the old folks. Which of these views do you favor?" In this case you have put the arguments into the mouths of third parties, and the interviewee feels free from any influence that you exert as a news-gatherer. He is on his own.

What about the "middle-of-the-road" type of interviewee? He doesn't say "yes" and he doesn't say "no." So you may ask, "Do you think that state taxes are too high, too low, or about right?" By giving him three alternatives, you have given him more freedom in his choices. If he answers, "About right," you will be able to ask questions to bring out the reasons for his reply.

The type of interviewee who can respond more quickly when given a number of alternatives is well known. Some researchers believe that most persons are unable to keep as many as five or six items clearly in mind at once. This does not mean that you limit the alternative statements to six. As in other questioning techniques, you must decide upon the number of alternatives according to the intelligence and personality of the interviewee, the specific issue, how the alternatives are worded, the interest of the person in the issue, and other pertinent factors. S. L. Payne notes that ". . . if folks are going to guess, they reason that the extremes are not very likely to be the correct answers."

On occasion you seek to know how intensely the person feels about an idea. Perhaps Mr. K has answered your question, but he showed no great amount of emotion in his response. Then you may pursue the topic further and ask, "How much difference do you feel this proposed ordinance to close movie houses on Sunday would make in church attendance—a lot, quite a bit, not very much, or none?" Your question will probably elicit an answer indicating the intensity of his feeling on the subject.

Can you combine several types of questions to produce one rounded appraisal? George Gallup has labeled one particular combination of polling questions the "quintamensional plan of question design," because it approaches any topic from five different directions. Although this type of questioning is not adapted to all interviewing situations, the reporter can keep these five elements in mind—awareness of or familiarity with the issue, expression of individual attitudes, reactions to the specific proposal, reasons for these reactions, and intensity of feeling.

Once your interviewee is "warmed up," he may wander off the subject. He may be interrupted by a phone call. His secretary may break in with routine business. You need not mind these interruptions. "Welcome them," says Marguerite Henry, in *Writer's Digest*. "Welcome these intermissions as an opportunity to repeat his pivotal remarks until you know them like a poll parrot."

Your knowledge of human nature will be of great help in deciding what attitude on your part will bring forth the desired response from the interviewee. At times, you must be more hopeful and optimistic than the person to whom you are talking. Again, you must be decidedly pessimistic about a pet scheme being promoted by your interviewee. By knowing your goal, you can isolate the main issues and determine the mood and techniques needed to make the most of the situation.

What can you do when you feel that a person is evading the truth? The lawyer often solves this problem by selecting the weakest points of the story told by the witness. Francis L. Wellman, in his book, *The Art of Cross-Examination,* advises: "Do not ask your questions in logical order, lest he invent conveniently as he goes along; but dodge him about in his story and pin him down to precise answers on all the accidental circumstances indirectly associated with the main narrative." Furthermore, the lawyer asks his questions rapidly. If he can do this skillfully, the evasive witness is almost certain to land in a maze of self-contradictions. Similarly, a person whom you are interviewing isn't likely to be able to invent answers as fast as you can frame questions.

Your interviewee will talk more freely if you show an interest in what he says. As a matter of fact, the man you thought would be a reluctant interviewee often becomes voluble just because the reporter is a good listener. Robert M. Neal reminds us that "A yawny, ceiling-gazing reporter is no spur to loquacity." Eager listening will help you in another way: by following what is being said closely, your chances of misunderstanding and misquoting are reduced.

Perhaps your interviewee explains that he would like to think the situation over. "Then I'll get in touch with you," he says. In that case you may be able to use this device: "The city editor is very anxious to get this story this afternoon," you declare. "He plans to give it space on page one. Now a lot of things could happen in a week—it might be just a little item by then." This technique usually brings results.

Always remember that each person is subject to control. Every man has a psychological nature which reacts in a specific manner whenever certain ideas or objects are brought to his attention. It is your job to discover which "buttons" to push. To get a man to react in a desired way, Abram Lipsky states in *Man, The Puppet*, the manipulator "must be a master of a technique of applying the proper irritant—for presenting the most moving ideas, and also upon occasion making the human mechanism whose reaction is craved more than ordinarily sensitive."

Your interviewee is talking, you are taking notes, and everything is moving smoothly. He makes a mistake in grammar. Generally, you make the correction when you write your story. Rarely does anyone talk for any length of time without tangling an occasional subject and verb, mislaying a pronoun, or splitting an infinitive. You must use judgment in reporting conversational lapses in grammar. You would never, for instance, attribute the same kind of diction to Dizzy Dean and Bishop Gonser. Remember the advice of dramatists: Keep the person "in character."

As a reporter, you have a powerful psychological factor in your favor. If you are following a news tip, you have a perfect right to find a person and talk with him. Anyone who is in public life or who depends on public support —officeholders, actors, athletes, musicians, dancers, and the like—realize the power of the press and respect it. This does not mean that you are free to use extreme measures in every tough interviewing situation. You must be guided by your common sense and your understanding of what constitutes public interest in deciding when to threaten and when to cajole. You must be tactfully aggressive.

You must use all of your creative ability when you prepare questions for lecturers, concert singers, and others who travel most of the time. They have acquired "interview fatigue." They are tired of hearing stock questions day after day. Therefore, it behooves you to stretch your imaginative muscles before the interview. Use your ingenuity and start generating ideas for questions. Through persistent use you can develop this ability. Devise fascinating questions, and you will be surprised to see how the "much-interviewed" people will respond.

Your questions are more than mere inquiries—they are professional procedures used to obtain information. Many questions are direct queries, but some are not. Other types include questions for affirmation or denial, the question asked as a restatement for clarification, questions used in cross-examination, the rhetorical question, and the leading question.

Do silences during an interview annoy you? They need not. Rather than rushing in to fill a vacuum with words, try to discover the cause of the interviewee's inability or reluctance to talk. Perhaps the subject under discussion has been exhausted. Maybe the silence indicates an emotional block. Then the interviewee may say, "You know, this is terribly embarrassing to me but here's what really happened. . . ." He regains his poise and continues. If the person becomes emotionally upset, you may find it wise not to force the conversation further along the lines that evoked that response. Rather, you may wish to direct the conversation into a new channel. In her *Essentials in Interviewing,* Anne F. Fenlason says that "The interviewer who feels he must fill every void of silence should know that his eagerness to talk is usually caused by concern about his own comfort rather than concern for his client."

Pauses may be all right when there is ample time, but what about the limited-period situation? Even here, much of the success of the interview depends upon the timing—adjusting the tempo of the situation to that of the interviewee. Even when you must catch someone on the run, you will find that an easy, unhurried manner is usually the most productive.

Sometimes you must thrust a question so unexpectedly that the person answers before he has time to think it over or refuse to reply. You have heard that the university football coach has resigned to accept another job. You're certain that your tip is correct. You do not ask the president of the university if Coach Smith has resigned, because it might bring the reply that he has not. Instead, you say, "President Jones, this is Tom Brown of the *Gazette*. Will a successor to Coach Smith be named at the next meeting of the board of regents?" Then the answer may come right back, "Yes, we'll probably name his successor at the July meeting." Your strategy has worked. It will prove easy enough to get additional information on the entire situation.

Then there is the day when you must write a story from unanswered questions. You may include in the story the questions which were asked but not answered. There is also the situation in which you cannot get in touch with the person you are seeking to interview. In that case you can state that he is absent from his office as reported by his associates, that he could not be reached by telephone, that he is spending five days on a fishing trip in Minnesota, or that he has not been seen at his clubs. Warning: Do not write a story that implies that the person disappeared in a mysterious fashion. Avoid any deduction which might suggest wrongdoing.

Sometimes it is best for you to assume a "poker face." You do not show excitement about the information, because if you do give any indication of its importance, your informant may become reticent. Why? "He may be startled by his own story," William E. Hall of the *Toledo Blade* says. Your informant may envision the story spread across the front page in huge headlines. Sensing this situation, he may decide to keep quiet or call in other reporters and tell them also. By talking casually with him and getting the facts in a rather noncommittal fashion, you often obtain an exclusive story. Keep your informant on the track, get the angles you want, but guard against an excited enthusiasm. If you give any indication of the importance of the story, your source may decide that the story should be given to all reporters. Remember to maintain a calm exterior if you want to keep your story exclusive.

What can you do if your interviewee refuses to answer questions bearing directly upon the story? One successful method of getting facts in this situation is to ask questions parallel to the main subject. By using indirect means, you may get enough material for a story. But don't be too hasty and jump at conclusions. Be especially careful in stories involving defamatory situations not to libel anyone.

Stories concerning politics and sports are often based on deductions and inferences. The skillful political reporter explains what the facts mean, what the trends are, what the issues imply, and the probable results of such conditions. He must have intelligence to "see through" political humbug or he will be "taken in" by political maneuvers.

When you feel that the interviewee is wavering, trying to postpone an answer, or becoming more reticent, you may revive his interest by using the "why" technique. It works like this. If he is undecided about commenting on certain issues or answering questions, ask him why. He may struggle to answer your "why." He may find it difficult to put his answer into words. Observe this example:

Mr. Tycoon: "I'll think it over."

Reporter: "Why?"

Mr. Tycoon: "Well—I—uh—it seems like the only thing to do under the circumstances."

In using the "why" technique, you may bring out certain objections. Keep him answering your "why's" and you will probably learn the real reason for his reluctance to talk further. Under your questioning perhaps he finally says, "I suppose this is news, but I'm afraid that some of our staff members will think I am a publicity hound in releasing these facts."

Reporter: "Is that your only reason for not giving me the facts?"

It's How You Bait the Hook

Mr. Tycoon: "Yes, that's the only reason."

Now that he has committed himself, you may say, "You are the executive head of your organization. As such, your views are newsworthy. As the chief executive, you speak for the organization. By your releasing these facts, your entire organization—staff members, stockholders, board members, and customers—will be benefited. Naturally, you want your company to keep its place of leadership. Now, you say that as the first step in simplifying the corporate structure of your organization, the principal subsidiaries engaged in mining and steel production, fabrication, and distribution will be merged soon into one subsidiary. When will that take place?" Then you get your story.

What is the best way of questioning a suspect in a crime? An important technique is to stress the fact that you are not trying to "pin something on him." You might explain that you are trying to eliminate him as a suspect, you want to publish his side. W. R. Kidd in his book, *Police Interrogation,* suggests another approach: "You may tell him that he doesn't have to talk if he doesn't want to, but if he does want to talk, nothing will stop him. You can assure him that you will be delighted if his story establishes his innocence."

Let me remind you of this basic truth: Be wary of yourself as a questioner. You want to make the query clear to the respondent, but even before that stage is reached, you must be sure that you understand the question yourself. If you go off half-cocked, asking a vague question, then you are almost certain to receive a vague answer. You must first define the issue for yourself. Determine exactly what you want to learn and why. Then phrase the question in words that will be understood by the interviewee. Ask yourself the questions you plan to pose, and you are more likely to make them meaningful to your respondent.

You must be attentive and alert to comments which might be featured in your story. In an article in *Writer's Di-*

gest, Frank A. Dickson, Jr., advises reporters to "keep your ears alert for a 'lead,' or the opening—which must be compelling and attractive if the author hopes to ring the bell. For an apparently trivial remark, such as a random shot, might develop into the main idea of the whole story."

Ninety-nine reporters out of one hundred—when they want their subjects to talk—emphasize what will be gained through their response. This is a strong approach. It works in countless situations. But there is another appeal, often forgotten, that is also compelling. Most of you agree with the late Chauncey Depew's statement, "I wouldn't sit up all of one night to make a hundred dollars; but I'd be willing to stay up three nights in a row, if need be, to keep from losing a hundred dollars." Your interviewee may remain unmoved when you tell him how much he will gain from the forthcoming story, but point out what he is losing by inaction, and see what happens. Be sure that words like "guard," "protect," "keep," and similar ones are accented in your questions.

"How many questions shall I ask?" You alone can determine the number. The total will depend upon the time allotted for the interview, the extent of the area to be covered in the questioning, the response speed of the interviewee, and other factors. Some reporters ask too many questions; others do not ask enough. The best thing for you to do is to study your own tendency—too many or not enough—and then seek to improve your methods. Too many questions may confuse the informant, while too few place too much burden on him and may leave important topics without comments.

In certain types of interviewing, you may be called upon to give advice and offer suggestions. When I was interviewing a Negro who had been sentenced to the electric chair, he asked me, "What will they do with my body if my relatives don't come after it?" It was easy enough to tell him to discuss the matter with the prison chaplain. How far the reporter should go in giving advice is always a problem and requires careful consideration in each instance.

Any celebrity who must face the press day after day, perhaps for weeks at a time, may become press-weary. As a result, it isn't easy to see some important people. Years ago a reporter tried to see Fritz Kreisler, but was not admitted. This reporter had an idea: Why not slip back stage during the last encore number? She did, just as Mr. Kreisler was entering his dressing room, she said, "I'm interested in knowing one thing about your violin?" Did he respond? Yes, indeed. Although he would not talk about himself, he would talk about his violin. Soon he was being interviewed and enjoying it.

How should you ask embarrassing or intimate questions? Here again, the manner depends upon the major topic, the personality, the occasion, and related factors. If Herbert Kintner does not wish to tell what he will do with the $3,000 prize money won at the Community Day program, then about all you can do is thank him and conclude the interview. His reticence must be respected. But if the topic is of public import, the reporter has both justification and obligation for stating that the interviewee was silent. Chief of Police Womeresley won't discuss council member Smith's complaint that police should keep a closer watch on taverns after midnight? Present the chief's refusal, but do it fairly by stating the question as well as the refusal to answer.

It is well to remember that embarrassing queries should be made with the same consideration you would like to receive under similar circumstances. "When the reporter is forced to ask such questions," Donald D. Hoover says in *Copy!*, "he should not forget that courtesy will leave a much better taste in everyone's mouth than an attempt at bluffing or 'beating down' the other person."

Where conditions make hasty interviewing necessary, as when a celebrity is arriving in a large crowd, know in advance what kind of statement you would prefer having and pop your questions clearly and convincingly. One of my most enjoyable interviews was talking with Madame Schumann-Heink in the taxi which rushed us from her hotel to the auditorium where she was to give a concert. When time is short, you must plan to make every minute count.

And then there are days when your city editor gets ideas. You know the kind—"Find out how many persons sleep in pajamas and how many sleep in the nude." If office orders make it necessary to ask banal questions, Russell S. Campbell of the *Indianapolis* (Indiana) *Star* says, "At least have the grace to admit that 'I know this is pretty silly, but if you can answer it, I would appreciate it.' "

Your success in interviewing is often dependent upon your friends. Here is an example of how you can use those friendships. Your newspaper is on the trail of a major story and you must be very judicious in deciding which of your news sources you are going to approach. You pick out a friend who should know what is going on and say something like this: "The office has gotten wind of a certain situation and is going to publish a story about it. I know you won't like it, but I can't do anything about it; so how about helping me since it's going to appear anyway?" A word of caution: These tactics will produce once in a while, but they should not be overworked.

On occasion, your respondent will indicate that your questions mark the first time certain matters have been brought to his attention. As a result, his thoughts on the subject are not crystallized and he cannot be articulate immediately. Thus you may find him thinking out loud before giving his answer: "Well-ll-l-, I hardly know . . . ." This is just an introductory phrase, a mulling through in his mind, preparatory to the expression of his real opinion. When this happens, do not push ahead too fast. Give each person a bona-fide chance to come to a decision.

The best interviews are kept on a conversational plane. This means that you should know your questions so well that you don't have to "read" them; rather, you can "ask" them as if they were extemporaneous. Keep the interview moving along smoothly. You may ask the next question while jotting down the answer to the previous one. In this way the interviewee can be framing his answer instead of spending idle moments waiting for you.

What about the smart aleck? What about the person who talks too much? In each instance, just cut him off politely with something like this: "That's an interesting reaction. Now, I'd like to know your comments on this question—."

You cannot separate a person's language from his personality. That is why it is important to record the interviewee's answer or comments in his own words. Watch for slang and colorful expressions. Earl Wilson was interviewing Groucho Marx in Larue's in Hollywood. Groucho motioned to a waiter and said, "Have you any milk-fed chicken? Well, milk one and bring it in." Such lines come easily for the funny man.

Here is a nervous person. He has the jitters. His answers do not come at all, or they may tumble out two or three at a time. Worse than that, the answer may be a "yes" and a "no" together. Then he may say, "I don't know." Two techniques are important in questioning this type of person: First, deal gently and be patient. Second, help and encourage him.

What about Mr. Last Word? You know him—he knows it all. He is the positive type; he is not likely to change anything he has said even though he has been mistaken. Here is a plan worth trying. By carefully phrasing your statements, you may lead him by small degrees to modify what he has said. Even such questions as "How do you know?" may cause him to crackle right back, "I know because I know." Try to understand what lies back of actions that are unusual. Be on the alert for tell-tale trifles which reveal traits of character. Is he clever or stupid? Would it be dangerous to praise him? What are some of the habits which control him? By discovering some clues to his character, you can use questioning techniques which are more likely to bring about the desired response.

Use a touch of humor as relief from the stiff question-and-answer routine. To begin with, it relaxes both the writer and the person to whom he is talking. Then it gives a bit of variety to what might be a rather perfunctory or formal situation. Tell a joke on yourself. Make a pun. Do, however, avoid the long, detailed story. Avoid telling one which might offend the other person. And do not drag in a story or joke, saying to yourself, "This whole thing is getting pretty dry so I'd better tell him my latest story." And don't forget, he may have a favorite story of his own. You may know what it's going to be before he starts, but he tells it again. The way you react to this particular ordeal really reveals whether or not you have a sense of humor.

Unexpected answers will often give you good ammunition for bright features. A reporter boarded the train carrying the Notre Dame team to the Southern Methodist game. Looking for a new slant on a story, he said to the student manager, "I understand that you carry a chaplain to pray for the team." "That's right," the manager answered. "Then would you mind introducing me to him?" the newspaperman asked. And the manager replied, "Be glad to. Which one do you want, the offensive chaplain or the defensive chaplain?"

Hy Gardner, of the *New York Herald Tribune,* while interviewing Sir Thomas Beecham, conductor of the Royal Philharmonic Orchestra, asked the famed leader, "Why do you refuse to hire female musicians?" "If they're pretty, they distract my male musicians," he said. "If they're not pretty, they distract me!"

Avoid suggesting negative answers in your questions. Yandell C. Cline once made a study of questions used by reporters and found that with a little more care and thought in phrasing the queries, the results were improved. In reporting the results of his investigation in *Editor and Publisher,* he related: "We found that 'Do you mind if I quote you?' was not nearly as productive of a bang-up news story as some remark such as 'That's fine, I'll quote you on that.'" He continued: "If the reporter asks the informant if he *minds* being quoted, the fact that perhaps he should *mind* is suggested to him. The question 'Would you care to give your name and age?' is not nearly so effective as 'Now give me your name and age, please.'"

An alert newsman ordinarily makes mental notes during conversations. Does the personality of the interviewee impress you? Is he frank and straightforward? Is he imaginative? Does he understand the significance of his remarks? What are his outstanding characteristics? Does he have any unique mannerisms? These are samples of the thoughts which a reporter should have in the back of his mind while talking with an interviewee.

Have you ever covered an event which seemed to tell itself? During a recent CBS series, "You and the Press," Meyer Berger of the *New York Times* told Quincy Howe and the radio audience: "Whenever I feel a story telling itself, I always avoid asking questions. That's a hard thing to learn, but you get the atmosphere better; people act more naturally. [He recalled three of his war stories: a night on a train with the first load of wounded returned from Africa and Sicily; the reactions of 1,300 men taken off the front lines for brief respite on account of special heroism; and a report on the blind veterans at Valley Forge General Hospital.] The murmurs, the little gestures, the reactions to common sights of men who hadn't been home in three years made a pretty powerful document that called for no questioning. It told itself."

Because most persons want to appear at their best in interviews, sometimes they stretch the truth. Furthermore, they are likely to be very quick with their answers. Dr. Melvin S. Hattwick, who has studied the psychological factors in advertising, advises that "On questions of income, position in the community, and the like, the tendency is to give answers which set the interviewee on a higher level."

You may find your interviewee giving inconsistent facts, figures, or opinions. Perhaps this is unintentional; or perhaps he has only a partial knowledge of the facts; or he may have a tendency to generalize. Remember that the memory of man is a highly selective mechanism and that his experiences have been subject to certain processes of selectivity and assimilation. You should note all of the answers, however, because they are clues to beliefs and behavior. In his book, *Social Discovery*, Eduard C. Lindeman reminds you to pay attention to a person's answers, even though false, because what is "in a person's 'mind' may or may not be true, but it is the sum total of his rationalizations upon which his life has proceeded."

What if the person interviewed utters contradictory statements? How does this situation affect the type of questions you will use? First of all, assume that the misstatement was unintentional. Then you may use the check question, as, for example: "Did you say that the Australian unionist has awakened to the fact that immigration does not take work from him, but makes work for him?" And your interviewee probably answers, "Yes, that's right." Another method of checking the contradictory statement is to approach the subject from a new angle.

If the misstatement was not unintentional, you may have proceeded too rapidly. Or perhaps the interviewee is not "mentally organized" well enough to give us the true facts. Be very careful in trying to catch him in a misstatement. In most instances, *rapport* is destroyed because your respondent becomes both embarrassed and confused.

Often Mr. Milquetoast and others of his tribe accompany their answers with a "What do you think?" or "Am I right?" You may pass the question off easily most of the time by stressing that it is his opinion that you want, that it is his view which will be of interest to readers.

Remember that an interview during business hours should not be regarded as a social call. If, in "breaking the ice" during the opening moments, you note that the interviewee shows impatience, and if your deadline isn't too near, you might suggest another appointment at a more opportune time.

Tricky methods to obtain information rarely ever succeed. The person who has achieved fame as an explorer, executive, or administrator, is not naïve enough to be deceived into giving confidential information. Moving down the ladder, you will discover that employees whom you contact usually see through attempted deception and resent having their intelligence underestimated.

Trick questions may backfire. While serving as secretary of defense, General George C. Marshall was harried by a reporter who asked long, misleading questions in an obvious effort to trick him into making an imprudent statement. Patiently, the General would sift the facts from these confusing queries and answer as best he could. This simply encouraged the reporter to ask more involved questions. Finally, after he had completed answering one of his longest and trickiest queries, General Marshall gave him a weary smile. "Would you mind," he said pleasantly, "repeating what you have just tried to say?"

You must guard against setting up blocks along the road to your goal by asking confusing questions or two or three questions at once: "Where did you find the body? How did it look? Whom did you call?" Each of these is a separate query, and the interviewee should be given a chance to answer each separately. Undoubtedly he would have given the answers to your questions in the normal course of telling his story had you not interrupted.

Many persons respond normally to questions in the opening of the interview only to become emotionally upset as they discuss crises. A person may laugh. He may blush. He may weep. And then he may become reticent. You should act promptly to avoid losing an important part of the story. Remember to build up *rapport*. You may branch out into other fields with your questions and then use a less direct line of approach to the subject later. You may lessen tensions by showing sympathetic interest, complimenting good performance, and in other ways demonstrating that you appreciate his position.

Today you interviewed Jim Turnesa after he won the national P. G. A. golf championship. He talks with ease. You won't have any problems. Tomorrow night you may be sent to interview a woman who is charged with selling narcotics to junior high school students. She refuses to talk. Obviously, some subjects are more difficult to talk about than others. The interviewee may be unable or reluctant to express himself, he may be inarticulate at points, or he may have language difficulties. As the reporter, you should come to the rescue with the required expression or any other aid which will help him preserve his poise.

You are nearing the end of the interview, but you want to be certain that you have your facts and opinions exactly right. If you like, you can repeat all important questions. For instance, you may ask: "It is your opinion, then, that teaching techniques in most schools today are adapted for adults, but not for children. You believe that few classroom activities are conducted on the basis of children's interests."

Another form of review is this: "It is true, isn't it, that you were forty-two years of age when you enrolled as a freshman at the university, and nine years later you were selected chairman of the department of history?"

Another form of reiteration is: "Then, Mr. Davenport, you believe that American policy cannot be solved in purely defensive terms. Is that right?"

An example of still another: "A few moments ago

you stated that the average time which respondents said they spent reading each issue of the newspaper was 43.1 minutes, or 42.8 for the men and 43.5 for the women. Are those the correct figures?"

You might try this approach: "And so, Dr. Harper, I may say that you have hoped that the Russians have not developed such a process? And, by the way, was it *nineteen* years ago that you first joined the staff of the Bureau of Standards?"

Now quickly, let's run the reel backwards and take a second look: (1) If your questions are to bring the desired answers, you must establish a common meeting ground with your interviewee. (2) Gear your questions to an individual. (3) Decide which types of questions will fit the specific situation. (4) Phrase your questions in the language of the interviewee. (5) Give some attention to the degree of feeling shown in the answers. (6) Be prepared to adapt your attitude so that the person responds in the desired way. (7) Avoid any appearance of talking down to those whom you interview. (8) Be eager to help your interviewee. (9) Avoid trick questions. (10) Use simple words and keep the questions as brief as possible. (11) Avoid stock questions in interviewing celebrities who are interviewed regularly. (12) Be ready to write a story from unanswered questions. (13) Talk casually and get the facts in a rather noncommittal fashion, so that you won't excite the interviewee and can keep your story exclusive. (14) Be courteous even in asking embarrassing or intimate questions. (15) Keep the interview on a conversational plane. (16) Avoid suggesting negative answers to your questions. (17) Watch for inconsistencies in facts, figures, and opinions. (18) Work fast to re-establish *rapport* when it is weakened or destroyed. (19) Repeat important questions if you want to make sure that you have the answers exactly right. (20) Always question yourself about your questions.

Any further questions?

7
Listen to the Experts

WHAT ARE THE DIFFERENCES between the expert interviewer and the cub reporter? You could list many devices
and abilities which the skilled newsman uses that the novice
may not even think important. After all is said and done, it is
the know-how—the specific and minute techniques—that you
find in the polished performer. By some peculiar magic, he
gets more than facts and comments from an interviewee.
Coupled with that ability, he has a news sense, a sense of
seeing something exciting even in drab human experiences.

"Good interviews are tough to get," you say. And
you are right. Fortunately, you will get over that feeling to
a great degree when you realize that no one has all the
answers. Top-flight interviewing, you see, consists of a lot
of answers all put together—answers you will get from reading, observation, planning, practicing, evaluating, and im-
proving—and from watching the experts in action.

It may surprise you to know that even you, though
you feel somewhat "green" technically, have some of the
answers. How does this happen? To begin with you like people or you would not be a wordsmith. You have watched
people and wondered about them. You have lived with people up and down Main Street. And best of all, you get out
among them to see and learn and remember. You have known
all along that you must understand people before you can

gain any facility in handling them. And because you want to step up your interviewing skills, you will keep adding to your stock of workable strategies.

You can shorten the road to success in interviewing in two ways: first, through experience, and secondly, by studying the methods used by the experts.

You can't succeed—you can't increase your ability— if you are a prima donna about your work. What is more, you must go out and meet people face to face. A good interviewer is never satisfied. He knows that he cannot possibly be perfect either in the situation or in his copy, but he works to do as successful a job as possible. To learn, one must do.

Next, you will strengthen your methods by keeping an eye on the experts. They have developed qualities, skills, and techniques which you can use. Give special attention to their (1) planning, (2) approaches, (3) techniques of questioning, (4) special methods, and (5) results.

The methods of top-flight writers vary. In fact, such writers often disagree on the techniques of influencing the thoughts and behavior of interviewees. How does this happen? Because there is no one best answer to any interviewing problem. Basically, you can use certain workable principles in almost any situation. Most of these principles are simple. The expert uses these basic strategies plus special methods of his own—methods which often make the difference between success and failure. His "plus" factors are worth knowing and remembering.

In the following pages, the experts discuss their individual methods and their application of them. You will find it well worth your while to study them carefully.

"State advantages to interviewee"

Arthur Krock, Washington Bureau,
The New York Times

1. I don't take notes. Thus far my memory has not

failed me, though I hasten to make notes as soon as I am out of sight of the person interviewed. If the interview is by telephone, of course, I do make notes, but necessarily they are sketchy.

2. If statistics are involved, I find some reason to have them repeated, to lodge them more firmly in my memory.

3. With a reticent subject I merely state what I consider to be the advantages to him and to the public of the information I seek. Most of the time it is sufficient.

4. The only "strategy" I use is not to frighten off the subject by indicating that he has told me something of greater importance than he realizes. For instance: when a public official in March, 1933, interrupted my questioning on another matter by asking me if I didn't think it was a "good step about the gold," I merely said I did—not expanding on the fact that this could only mean the United States was going off the gold standard and that this was earth-shaking and completely fresh news.

5. The best "technique" I have discovered, when the subject wants to be interviewed or has been persuaded, is to write out the questions and let him write out the answers, if he chooses, and there is time for it.

"Keep on the main trail"

Roy Stewart, Washington Bureau,
The Daily Oklahoman

Having interviewed all types of persons for quite a spell, the only general conclusion I have is that no yard-stick will measure the mass—each individual and the conditions around each interview form a separate cut-out most difficult to put into a broad pattern.

For a straight story, the most valuable starter is to have questions ready in your mind to ask because businessmen or politicians without a specific personal thing they're trying to put over must be probed by direct questions in order to get direct answers.

When you know what you are after—in other words, know something of what the story is, provided you can pin someone down to talk about it—you had better know enough about it to have some intelligence in keeping on the main trail. The background you often get from someone else besides your main suspect, or from bits of information—even tangents to your idea—which have previously been published or which are knowledge of a reputable person not authorized to talk on your subject for publication.

You can't have any squeamishness about digging for information if you really want a story. If you want personal information on an individual who has been killed, for instance, and no one but the family is available to supply that information—being unaware of the fatality at that point —you have to be callous enough to say, "We hear he has had an accident and when we learn more we will tell you," and proceed with your questions.

The motives of revenge, greed, and the desire for self-glory are paramount in getting people to talk, but those elements are present in the persons. You do not supply them; you just recognize them.

People in a state of shock will talk when they will clam up later: the family of a murdered daughter at Sand Springs, for instance, was bitter amidst natural grief the day of the happening. The man who committed the crime was still in a high state of some kind in the jail before the inevitable letdown hit him, so he was willing to talk. Both those stories poured out; few questions were needed.

Aimless-sounding chatter, probing to find a person's interest or special enthusiasms, seem time wasting, but have a place because some people face an interviewer like they do a camera—they freeze up. Conversational knowledge of the subject you are really after, at least the interviewee's part in it, is a great help. So is a mutual acquaintanceship because that puts one in a friendly atmosphere to start with.

"Keep them to the point"

LOWELL M. LIMPUS, chief, U.N. Bureau,
The New York News

In my opinion, most people with whom we deal fall into two broad general classifications:

1. people who want to be interviewed;
2. people who don't want to be interviewed.

There are two sub-classifications under each, and they may be organized as follows:

1. experienced interviewees;
2. inexperienced interviewees.

Experienced interviewees, who want to be interviewed, are a lead-pipe cinch, nine times out of ten. The experienced type includes statesmen, public officials, diplomats, civic leaders, and press agents. When they want to be interviewed, it usually means they've got something to sell and, being experienced, they've usually got their selling talk all organized and ready to go—frequently backed up by mimeographed statements prepared in advance. They're all set to suggest questions themselves, if the reporter misses a point. (Occasionally they may pose as reluctant, but you can spot that pose easily enough; ask the guy for a picture—if he has one ready, he's willing all right.)

Experienced interviewees who don't want to be interviewed are a much harder nut to crack. They include most army and navy officers of high rank, public officials under investigation, politicians who haven't yet decided which way the cat is going to jump, and diplomats who have to consult their governments before they know where they stand. These people are difficult to handle, and the trick is to slip up on them if humanly possible. That calls for preparation. It includes looking up in advance their personal hobbies, background, and records, upon which a little judicious flattery may be based. It pays to get an introduction from a mutual friend. If possible, you lead into the interview by a discussion of something about which the subject is interested, and when you get him talking, *let him talk.* Avoid direct questions, but gradually steer the conversation into the course you want it to follow. *Take no visible notes.*

With this type and all inexperienced interviewees, I never permit them to see me take a single note, if possible. My own pet gag is to stroll in carrying a copy of the community's most conservative newspaper, carelessly folded so that a big department store ad with lots of white space is on the under-side. I have a small pencil already palmed. If possible, I seat myself across the desk from the interviewee, drop the paper down on one knee (below the level of the desk so he can't see it), slip out my pencil, and start taking notes on the white paper as soon as he begins talking. He doesn't realize I'm doing so and so escapes the attacks of Buck Fever, which seize so many people when they suddenly realize their remarks are going to be embalmed in cold type. (More promising interviews have bogged down at sight of a pencil than most people realize.) In case the fever does develop, get the guy sore at something, as long as it isn't yourself. But never let him suspect you're taking notes while he's blowing off steam.

Inexperienced interviewees who want to be interviewed are fairly simple, but the big problem is to keep them to the point. If necessary, you can afford to be brusque with them, in order to avoid waste of time. If they resent it, calm them down by asking for a picture.

The inexperienced types who don't want to be interviewed can be trapped if you handle them carefully. The trick is to be sympathetic and make friends. If you're calling on them at home, praise their children and their pets, getting chummy with both if possible. Feel out their politics and agree with them. You can risk more flattery here than with the experienced type. An appeal to sympathy often works; tell 'em you may lose your job if you don't bring back something.

General rules for all four types include the following: (1) be very careful to reserve any questions that could prove offensive until you are ready to leave (or to be thrown out, as the case may be); (2) don't knock a rival paper—it may be his favorite; (3) when people finally begin to talk—don't interrupt. Let 'em talk, and save your questions until they run down.

You ask for a specific instance. I think the most difficult and perhaps the most successful interview I ever secured was with General Tomouki Yamashita, the Japanese commander, during his trial in Manila in 1945 and just before he was hanged as a war criminal. It took six weeks of patient work to set it up. I finally secured it by means of a long series of notes and letters, which had to be translated into Japanese and forwarded to him in his cell, after each day's hearing, through members of his defense counsel.

The basis of my appeal for the interview was that he was Japan's outstanding commander and owed it to his professional standing with posterity to clear up certain moot technical points about his campaigns while there was still time to do so. The idea evidently intrigued him, and he started sending me questions concerning the kind of points I had in mind. I secured expert advice and carefully framed answers, which almost demanded detailed explanations on large-scale maps. After a long series of exchanges, he invited me to his cell, where he and members of his staff could go over these points with me.

For two long hours I listened to detailed technical explanations of strategy and tactics, by which time Yamashita was in a pretty good humor. One question about how he learned these things led to a long discussion of his parentage, family, and education. A reference to religious training slipped into a request for more details about his boyhood brought out an exposition of his religious beliefs. They included a reference to the beauties of nature, and a little prodding on that line revealed that his personal hobby was growing chrysanthemums. By this time we had strayed away from technical matters, and we didn't come back to them until just before I left, when I finally risked the two questions that I feared might cause him to bristle. The first dealt with atrocities committed by troops under his command against civilians and American prisoners and the second was why he didn't commit hara-kari instead of surrendering. By then he wasn't inclined to bristle, but plunged into lengthy explanations of both points.

I think this episode illustrates several of my theories, but spare you the comment. In conclusion, the one thing that is most baffling to the patient interviewer is a kindly, persistent "No comment." When I encounter that, I always try to prod the subject into losing his temper, resorting even to direct insult as a last desperate measure. If that doesn't work, I'm licked. I wonder if anybody else knows how to solve it.

"Reporter must sell himself"

MAX K. GILSTRAP, chief, Central News Bureau, *The Christian Science Monitor*, Chicago

To click in an interview, the knowledgeable reporter should be able to probe the interviewee's thinking and background with searching and perceptive questioning. Equally important, he should be able to intersperse his questions with occasional cogent opinions of his own which will give the one interviewed something new to think about.

A reporter thus gains the respect of his subject, who will be much more likely to talk freely, with the feeling that what he says will be handled with care and understanding, rather than superficially or erroneously, which might place him in an unintelligent or ridiculous light.

The reporter, of course, should be well versed in

the background of the person he is to interview. Thus armed, he will be in a better position to skip over those details which can be obtained by reading and get to the fresh idea material which should be the meat of the interview.

The reporter, like the salesman, has to sell himself. He should be neat in appearance. He should exude controlled enthusiasm, coupled with a certain poise and dignity. His approach should be friendly, natural, and sincere. He should show a grasp of his subject and a decisiveness which indicates his recognition of the value of another's time.

A reticent person can be brought out frequently by a reference to something in which he is interested which may be entirely unrelated to the subject under discussion. An example of this occurred in an interview I had with E. H. "Boss" Crump of Memphis. Noting some Audubon bird prints lining the walls of Mr. Crump's hallway and a stuffed bird in his office, I spoke of my hobby of bird study as a former ranger-naturalist in the national parks. In fact, I produced a few bird sounds, to his surprise and delight.

As Mr. Crump relaxed from his characteristic formality, I changed the subject from birds to politics and he talked enthusiastically for two-and-one-half hours instead of the originally planned thirty minutes.

Another quality I would list as essential for the interviewing reporter is confidence. Confidence in himself. Confidence in his ability. Confidence in the worthiness of the task he is performing. Confidence in the belief that his subject appreciates the value of being interviewed.

The confident reporter starts at the "top" for his interviews. No one is too big for him. He heads for the office of the boss whose opinions usually ring with more authority and meaning than some third assistant. More likely than not the boss is available, since he probably got where he is partially by recognizing the important things such as having a proper public reflection of himself and his work.

"Scientists dislike foolish questions"

WALDEMAR KAEMPFFERT, science editor,
The New York Times

My experience in interviewing is limited to scientists, but I suppose that the principles that I have found useful apply with equal force to actors, lawyers, corporation presidents, bankers, and others in high and low places.

Nothing exasperates a scientist more than foolish questions. At a dinner in Paris, attended by Victor Hugo, the famous physicist Arago talked on comets. Like most literati, Hugo knew nothing about astronomy. So after having listened patiently, he asked, "But M. Arago, what is the soul of a comet?" The question was silly and meaningless. It is the kind of question that too many reporters ask of scientists as well as of statesmen.

A reporter ought to prepare himself for an interview. He must ask the right questions, and this he can do only by informing himself. So I make it a point to read what I can find about the person I must interview and also to read some of his papers. This saves much time. Moreover, the scientist is willing to talk more freely when he has someone before him who is apparently well informed. This was my experience with the late Sir Arthur S. Eddington, a devout Quaker who had his own idea of the relation of religion to science. He certainly let himself go with me.

Similar preparation proved to be of value in interviewing the late Franklin D. Roosevelt on his power policy. My interview was virtually written before I spent half an hour with him at Hyde Park on a summer afternoon. His conception of the social effects of the dissemination of high-voltage electric energy over a radius of two hundred miles from its source was not very clear. But the article dealt largely with these effects and justified his power policy. At that time the President could not be directly quoted, and all interviews had to be submitted to him for approval. I went off to Europe right after the interview had been approved. When I returned, I found that F. D. R. (or his ghost writer) had used most of my interview in a message to the World Power Congress, which was meeting in Washington at the time.

When the person interviewed is very important and his statements are bound to influence the thinking of many newspaper readers, it is always well to submit the interview for approval. This is good protection for the interviewer. Too often the great deny that they ever made statements attributed to them—what is called "corroborative denial" in newspaper circles. But when you have a letter approving the interview, there can be no denial.

Approved interviews are most important when it comes to dealing with medical men. They may not be directly quoted in an interview, because that would be a violation of something called "medical ethics," but what they say can be stated in the third person. Medicine is about the most ticklish subject that a science writer is called upon to handle. Thus the word "cure" must never be used by the reporter, but if the medico who is interviewed used the word, it is well to let the fact be known and say that it is his word.

Corporation presidents hem and haw and hate to commit themselves to anything except something of direct advertising or publicity value to the companies with which they are associated. When they have to weigh their words, they usually hand out a prepared statement. The practice has its merits. The great man cannot very well deny his own typewritten statement. Usually these statements are brilliantly noncommittal. It is hard to pin the corporation president down, except when it comes to quoting statistics; he is as elusive as a drop of mercury on a glass plate.

It is a pleasure to deal with scientists. They tell the truth. They are modest. They are as cautious as corporation presidents, but they do not hesitate to state boldly what conclusions they have reached after much experimenting and rumination. When they prove to be wrong, they come right out and say so. I have yet to meet the corporation president or the eminent politician who admits that he was wrong when he said so and so.

"Lay it on thick . . . sometimes"

WERNER RENBERG, City Desk,
The Dallas Morning News

Getting reticent persons to talk is something I do not face too often. Usually the persons I am assigned to interview are quite willing to talk, realizing they get their names and, perhaps, pictures in the paper. Or maybe it is the nature of Texans to talk. Reticent or not, the person I interview has to be caught off-guard. I like to chat about the weather or his trip (if he just got here)—in short, interests, acquaintances, or something. Anyway, the first thing you know, we are good friends. And before he knows it, he is talking about what I want to know. If it is a conservative doctor, hesitant to talk about himself or his work, I tell him that many people are interested in medicine and are eager to know what he thinks about this or that. Really? he might ask. And he starts to talk.

If I know a fellow is in on a big deal or has done something that may be a big story but that he doesn't want known, I don't ask him whether something is true. That is, not "Is it true that you beat your wife?" but, instead, "When did you beat your wife?" or something like that—a question that gives him no opportunity to deny. In such a situation, I usually try to know everything I can about the man and his deed. Overwhelmed about how much is known of what he thought secret, he may—usually does—start talking. Or I may, on purpose, tell one of the facts I know wrong. That will make him correct me, giving me the correct facts.

Often, I try to needle people into giving me answers

or joke them into it. I may impress upon them how important they are or how important what they are doing is. Usually, of course, I don't believe this. But most people like to have their ego built up. And for the sake of a good story, I lay it on thick. Of course, sometimes the opposite is true. Sometimes a fellow might not give me a story if he thought it is as important as I think or if he knew how very much I wanted it. Then I play as if I don't care, and twist a few facts out that way with haphazard questions.

I can say that usually good humor, an expression of interest, a desire to make the interviewed person comfortable (or at ease), and an attitude making him think he is doing the right thing by talking to me—these are what I would consider essential to a good interview. I think they would do equally well whether the subject be the President or the bearded lady at the zoo.

"Each human is an entity"

Edward J. Mowery, staff writer,
New York World-Telegram

I don't subscribe to the theory that there's one set technique or format in getting the most out of an interview. Conversely, it has been my experience that each human being is a separate, distinctly different entity who must, in a sense, be coddled and understood by an expert interviewer. Reticence is a thin veneer, in my book, which masks the person's hatred of your objective, fear of being booby-trapped, or in some instances an inferiority complex.

In twenty years interviewing the mighty and the mediocre, the ward-heeler and the murderer, the erudite and the purist, I've found that if the questioning is routed their way to put them at their best advantage (Call it flattery, if you will!), they'll talk. You asked for specific examples. I'm afraid that would take another book.

Specifically, however, in breaking the nation-wide dope racket, I ran across the usual gamut of officials, police, addicts, do-gooders, legislators, and dope traffickers. Each presented a problem. Each had an axe to grind. Each thoroughly distrusted *any* handling of their participation in drugs. The cop parried questions because he felt the blame for addiction was his, as did the legislator and the mayor. In this two-year battle to get the truth, I had to juggle each person's own problem and route the questioning toward his ego (to help clean up the mess), his resentment (at being suspect), etc. Mobsters, of course, are always wary of disclosing information that may bring underworld retribution. They, too, can be managed adroitly.

I'm reminded of the Bertram Campbell Case—the famed Wall Street broker wrongly convicted for forgery. I exonerated him because he let his hair down in the very first interview *after* I impressed upon him that he was a social scapegoat and owed it to other innocent men to tell how a lackadaisical D. A. is a menace to society. He blew the whistle on the D. A. (who by this time was the governor—Tom Dewey).

In another case involving an alleged poison murderer who had never been interviewed by the press and who had never taken the stand in his own defense in two trials, I again impressed upon him (Benjamin Feldman, Brooklyn) that the only chance he had to beat the chair at a third trial was for him to trace his life history from the time he was a child until he faced the Death House. I told him I'd try to ferret out every little incident benefiting him in the eyes of the third trial jury. I picked his brains along these lines and we came up with a pretty hair-raising first piece.

The D. A. reluctantly granted the interview under heavy guard in Raymond Street Jail. Feldman had to buck this atmosphere of belligerency in pouring out his heart. He knew that his words to me meant life or death. The D. A. polled the prospective trial jury to see if they read my piece and whether it warped their value as jurors. All professed not to have read the piece. *But . . .* they acquitted Feldman!

In the 1952 Revenue Bureau corruption series which ran in Scripps-Howard papers, the man spilling the sordid picture was the newly resigned King Committee chief investigator. Again, I had to be thoroughly familiar with his background, his likes and dislikes, etc., to be able to get the most out of him.

"Be sure interviewee knows who you are"

HUGH MORRIS, State Capital Bureau,
Louisville Courier Journal, Frankfort

In my book, the cardinal rules for successful interviewing are these:

1. *Never* accept any information "off the record."

When this term is used, I always stop the interview, explain that my business is to get information *on* the record. If the person you are interviewing means only for you to keep him out of the story, perhaps that can be done without injury either to the truth or to the facts.

2. *Always* be sure the person you are interviewing knows who you are, and that the information you are seeking is intended for publication.

"Cloak-and-dagger" reporters can get themselves in plenty of trouble. It has been my experience that most people will talk to a newsman for publication if he frankly tells them why he wants the information and what he intends to do with it.

In other words, "come clean" at the start of your interview. Doubtless there are some situations when a reporter cannot disclose his motives. Usually these instances are few and should be avoided as much as possible.

"*Know what you want*"

JOHN ROSENFIELD, amusements editor,
The Dallas Morning News

I have interviewed every conceivable type of personality in the last twenty-seven years and I still do not have a technique. Some subjects want the words put into their mouths; others want to do all the talking. Some do not want to be conscious of the interview; others under certain circumstances make prepared statements. On the other hand, there are a number of important people in the arts who are perfectly willing for me to invent the interview and make them say anything I think they should under the circumstances.

I believe the interviewer should have some notion of what he wants the interview to be. He certainly should be prepared to ask certain leading questions so the interview does not die on the vine. Many young reporters are so busy projecting their own personality in expressing themselves that the interview bears little resemblance to the subject. The experienced reporter is usually observant, quick to take in the moods and habits of his subject to adapt himself to them.

I believe the reader of the paper is as interested in the age, weight, shape, and personal appearance of the interviewee as he is in what is said, often nothing of importance. Frequently our interviews with motion picture stars are nothing more than personal impressions of the stars who had nothing to say worth wasting paper and type on.

"*Know one major field*"

HOUSTON WARING, editor,
Littleton (Colo.) *Independent*

I feel that the great weakness of the American system of interviewing is that we send the same man to get a story from a visiting economist, labor leader, physicist, or prime minister—and he probably does not have the background to interview more than one of these. It is my understanding that on the responsible British papers the interviewer has considerable knowledge of the subject in question. This probably makes for dull interviews, as the run-of-mine American reporter can write a more interesting, if not more helpful, story than a British specialist. At least we can require our reporters to acquaint themselves with one major field, such as education, religion, labor, social welfare, politics, etc. Then they will be somewhat prepared for the interviews they will conduct.

"Let him ramble"

GEORGE THIEM, Springfield Bureau,
Chicago Daily News

A good listener who shows genuine interest in what he is being told is necessary to draw out the person being interviewed.

Sometimes I've observed that the interviewee may be stimulated to tell more by exchanging bits of personal information with him.

You want to avoid any evidence of pumping the storyteller. Let him ramble; when he gets too far away from the thing you want, bring him back unobtrusively with a question or two that indicates you are really interested aside from getting the story.

There's no set rule. All people are different and your judgment or intuition should guide you in getting the facts.

"Get the subject relaxed"

VICTOR O. JONES, night editor,
The Boston Globe

The most important thing in an interview is to get the subject sufficiently relaxed so that he is literally "himself" and not a stereotype of everyone else who has ever submitted to an interview. This takes a good deal of personality on the part of the interviewer, who must be able to inspire confidence and a sort of friendship almost at first sight.

That's a pretty broad generalization. A detail that follows from it is that an interviewer must have a good memory for words, phrases, and expressions. He must, I say, have a memory because he should not use a notebook—that being one of the things which will make it difficult for the interviewee to be himself. But the exact words used by the subject are important not only on the score of accuracy, but for the character traits and mannerisms they bring out. Too many reporters lack this memory and will wind up making college professors and ball players sound alike.

Oh, there are a million and one other "tips," but I have no doubt that you are familiar with all of them. Besides the quotes, for instance, it's important to include a description of the subject, his clothes, his salient physical characteristics, his manner. I recall one interview, with some glamour girl, which even included the smell and very effectively!

"Ask the right questions"

EDWIN GUTHMAN,
The Seattle Times

Success of any interview depends upon the reporter's asking the right questions and persuading the person being interviewed to answer them. The reporter must win the trust and respect of the person he is interviewing. This can be done in a reasonably short time, if the reporter is firm but treats the person he is interviewing with courtesy and understanding—and if the reporter knows what he is talking about.

Keys to Successful Interviewing

I'd list three "Don'ts":

Don't go into an interview "cold."

Don't hesitate to ask any question, even if it might be most embarrassing. Most people will surprise you with their frankness.

Don't give up easily.

"Let the man talk himself out"

CARL E. LINDSTROM, managing editor,
The Hartford (Conn.) *Times*

Besides the usual questions, I always ask a job applicant what his hobbies are. A man's avocational interests are a tremendous asset to any newspaper.

Secondly, I let a man talk himself out. He is always prepared to put his best foot forward. When he has exhausted his prepared arguments, he will improvise. That is when he will reveal his weak points and you can best take his measure. He may also reveal some assets which he himself may not be aware of.

"Sound knowledge of the subject"

DAVID DIETZ, science editor,
Scripps-Howard Newspapers

Thirty-seven years in the newspaper business have convinced me that the most important thing in obtaining an interview is to have a sound knowledge of the subject to be discussed. The success of your interview will depend on whether or not you can inspire the person being interviewed with confidence. There is no substitute for intelligent questions.

You cannot, for example, interview an astronomer if he discovers in the first few minutes that you are unaware of the difference between a star and a planet.

146

"*Know something of the 'soft spots'*"

PAUL R. LEACH, Washington Bureau,
Knight Newspapers, Inc.

If I have time in advance of an appointment, I like to know something of the "soft spots" of the subject to be interviewed. Is he a fishing enthusiast? A historian in his reading? Is he a top golfer? Uppermost, of course, is the subject I want to interview him about. I note questions I want to put to him on that subject. The "soft spot" information is valuable in case your subject slows down on the main topic. Maybe you can revive his interest in talking by getting on to his hobby, then getting back for a fresh approach to the main topic.

I like to take notes in an interview, especially if the person is good at uttering quotable lines. But you occasionally run into a man who shies at a notebook. If you see that or sense it in him, put the notebook away and talk, trusting to memory to get what you want. It is essential, however, if you don't use a notebook, to make notes as quickly as possible after leaving him. You'll lose good stuff if you don't. Some interviewers like the provocative approach. That is, challenge your man, get him worked up. I think it is risky unless you know your man pretty well. He's liable to clam up if irritated. It's a mistake for an interviewer to talk much himself—tell the man what he himself thinks. Let the interviewed do the talking; your questions and comments should be designed to keep him talking, to amplify or clarify or explain his statements.

Mass Press conference: I don't like 'em, but they've become a fixture in public life. My practice in mass interviews has been to let others ask the questions while I listen, noting questions or answers which need amplification or explanation, or perhaps a touch of color that is lacking. I throw in my questions after the conference has progressed to the point where I want answers that I doubt I'm going to get otherwise. I may have specific questions in which only my papers would be interested. I reserve them for the time when the conference is slowing down. At a press conference I like to sit near two or three men I know will be asking interesting questions so that I can put in my nickel's worth when I see what they're driving at.

You ask how a reporter can make the most of an interview when it must be done on the spur of the moment. . . . You meet a man you had not known you were going to interview, and you sit down together, or catch him on the run. You make the rules for that as you go along.

Frequently an interview is only the beginning of a story. Your subject may make assertions that require checking with other persons. There may be a difference of fact or opinion which requires checking back to the original interviewed person. If the interviewed makes more or less serious charges against an individual, or gives one side of a controversial story, more interviews are necessary to round out a job.

"Spontaneous and friendly conversations"

Mary Handy, *The Christian Science Monitor,* Boston

I try to make friends of the people I interview. Once I had an interview with the European director of the Salzburg Seminar and with the American business manager of the seminar. After I had talked with them a while, and found the European director a delightful person—but not very precise in giving factual information—I began to figure out the sort of article I wanted to write. I arranged with the *Monitor* to give them a whole-page spread. And then I went about seeing them for a whole afternoon when we'd have plenty of time to talk.

I found prejudices they had against many Americans. I tried to convince them that since I had studied and lived abroad myself, I understood what they were working for. I did everything in my power—with jokes, and telling things that had happened to me—to make them feel that I was one of them. That my interests were their interests.

The more we got talking about what we felt deep within ourselves were the meaning and purpose of the seminar, the happier I was.

This is the kind of thing I always do. Every time I do a new interview, I make a new friend almost every time! I am as informal and natural as I can be. And I often volunteer things that I feel to make the man I'm interviewing realize that we're discussing something together. I find that I ask the questions I'm honestly interested in. And the more natural, sincere, and sympathetic I am, the more I get what they really feel.

I'm against formality of any kind. Interviews can be spontaneous and friendly conversations—with the other fellow giving most of the answers and telling how he feels—which most "other fellows" love to do.

If the subject is controversial and smacks of political intrigues—as often my interviews with school committee members and school administrators do—I get the people to talk off the record—volunteering some of my own off-the-record opinions—or asking for clarification. Then they begin to feel they can trust me.

And, of course, with making friends of interviewees you have to size up the value of what they say, whether you agree with it—and especially what is the policy of the paper toward what they have to say. If you seem naïve and simple on the outside, you have to be clever on the inside.

"Resist the off-the-record stuff"

JACK FOISIE, *The San Francisco Chronicle*

Preparation: If the reporter has time before his assignment he should bone up on the subject of the interview, and the field it deals in.

Keys to Successful Interviewing

Most general-assignment reporters have only a scant, finger-tip acquaintance with most subjects. If he is going to ask pertinent questions, and particularly timely questions, he should go to the clips, or to reference material.

And to draw upon color, he should look for biographical material on the person he's questioning.

That helps to get the interview going. To keep it going requires, sometimes, persistence by the reporter. Some interviewed persons are glib, but they don't really say much. Particularly if the questions go toward controversial subjects. In such a case, a reporter should hold his victim to a question until he gets a clear answer, a direct answer.

Don't be afraid to say: "Pardon me, Mr. Jones, but I don't understand your meaning. I want to express your thoughts accurately. Tell me again."

The big threat these days is that so many names in the news seek to hide behind off-the-record statements. They shift with the ease of a fluid-drive car. And they assume, without asking, that a reporter binds himself to such a commitment, even though they give the reporter no time to say so. And many reporters don't resist this subtle form of intimidation.

If you agree to off-the-record stuff, interrupt to say so and define the statements which you consider off, and which you consider on, the record. I personally usually resist the off-the-record stuff. I say: "Just a minute, Mr. Jones. If you want this off the record, I'll leave the room. When you are ready to talk on the record, call me back in." That normally tightens the reins on the flowing conversation, and he keeps on the record much of what he intended to say off the record.

"Do research for assignment"

MALCOLM BAUER, associate editor,
The Oregonian, Portland

150

The reporter should do research for any interview assignment, however trivial it may seem to him. There are innumerable sources for such information; the morgue clippings, magazine articles, "who's who" listings. This preparation should be organized in at least a few questions designed to draw from the subject comments worthy of publication.

It is to be deplored that the practices of newspaper work call for a story when the interview subject may really have no story. When confronted with such a situation, the honest reporter will not try to dress up his report or to build a sensation out of platitudes. Better say Mr. So-and-So liked the weather in Portland today than to put trimmings on views that have even less significance. This I know is a theory not popular among city editors who expect their reporters to produce on every assignment.

"Make interviewee feel at ease"

LEE BOND, Southwest Division news editor,
United Press, Dallas

The reporter's first task in an interview is to make the person he is interviewing feel at ease. Some persons are over-awed by newsmen and reticent. The reporter must get his subject to talking about himself. Ask him about his family; have the children had the mumps? Get yourself and your subject on some common ground. Ask your subject if he knows "so-and-so," if he has been to, say, New Orleans.

If the reporter is interviewing, say, a scientist, it's probably best for the reporter to explain that he would like the matter under discussion told in simple terms. "If I understand it," the reporter may say, "then I can write it so the public can understand it."

If you're interviewing a person, who, perhaps has been kicked about in the press, the reporter may say, "We want to tell your side in this controversy. Just tell me in your own words how you feel about this."

Keys to Successful Interviewing

"Casual, friendly approach"

CLARK PORTEOUS, *Memphis Press-Scimitar*

My stock in trade is supposed to be an ability to get people to talk and talk fully and freely, but it's an intangible sort of thing, and it's as much psychology as anything else, and difficult to explain. It boils down pretty simply to common sense.

I once heard my city editor say, "Porteous can get people to talk because he doesn't take notes, remembers everything they say, and they don't realize how much they're telling him, while if he took notes, it would scare them from talking." Another once said, "Porteous gets people to talk by taking careful and full notes; they know he's getting what they say right, and talk." So there you are.

Actually, there are times when you should and should not take notes. If you talk to a guy, say a policeman, a guy in the underworld, and often someone not accustomed to dealing with reporters, someone from whom you want information, I think it often helps not to take notes, let him talk, then jot down the gist of what he says when you leave him.

But if you talk to a celebrity, banker, businessman, governor, mayor, or someone else accustomed to meeting reporters, they are apt to have more confidence if you are taking down what they say, and will say, "Don't quote me on this, but," or that awful, "This is off the record," on portions of what they say they don't want attributed to them.

That takes care of note-taking. Now about modern interviewing, on an afternoon paper like mine, where you have to move fast, cover a lot of stories in near-by towns, etc., it's rapidly becoming a question of telephone interviewing. I think a friendly, easy approach, without trying to put officials on the spot, such as don't ask warden of prison, "How did you happen to let those prisoners get away," or "Tell me about the big jail break." Rather, you might say "How are you, Warden Smith, how's crops on the prison farm," or weather, etc. Sort of easy, conversational, then ask, "Understand you had a little trouble, or someone got away, have you got them yet," etc., put an optimistic note into question, don't try to blame, and they are apt to talk much more freely, or so I believe after eighteen years.

Another interview tip, if going to interview someone well known, a college president, say James B. Conant of Harvard, or other person in the news, a bit of preparation, if you have time, by reading through hurriedly stuff in morgue, being familiar with his latest statements and activities, and letting him see that you know the score will help get a better interview.

Another thing—you have to be a good listener. Too many reporters talk too much. That's good, to a point. You have to know how to prime the conversation, get the interviewee started, ask something now and then, but it's best to give your subject time to express his views, and not keep inflicting your own.

Also, doing a good job, quoting subject correctly, not letting him appear silly unless there is real point in it, straightening out minor grammatical lapses, etc., is a help. If person knows you'll quote him correctly on the sense of what he is saying, even if you do polish up his language a bit, and don't let him make a fool of himself for no reason, next time he's going to be much more willing to give.

Of course, one of the oldest gimmicks in the game, when talking to a reticent person, especially someone in trouble, jail, etc., and you want to write a helpful story, is to suggest answers. Such as a fellow who in a drunken brawl has stabbed his friend. "You guys were real good friends, huh?" Answer probably "Yeah." Your quote, "We were real good friends." But watch pitfalls of "You guys were like Damon and Pythias," and he says, "Yeah," and you use quote, and he obviously had never heard of Damon and Pythias.

Another good gimmick, I don't mind using, especially with doctors, scientists, and people who want to be exact, is to get a story and agree to read it back. This often helps the reporter on the technical sort of story, too. He gets it right.

"Carry on a casual conversation"

WILLIAM A. WHITE,
The Pittsburgh (Penn.) *Press*

I'm glad to be able to give you some of my ideas because it is something I've drilled into kids a lot over the years. I haven't had the job of interviewing a lot of greats or near-greats in recent years, so I'm a bit stale. My job now is to travel around, *à la* Ernie Pyle, writing a column about Pennsylvania and Pennsylvanians, but even before that I was on a desk so long that I almost forgot how to do it. Nevertheless, it is one of the spots where so many reporters fall down. And I can cite a case in point, which happened to a man who is now editor of one of America's greatest dailies. This is it:

The reporter went out to interview one of the Mellons, and no one of the Mellons was ever much for talking a lot to newspapermen. The reporter had a couple of stock questions—I don't know what they were—but nothing else. He asked one question. Mr. Mellon studied for a minute, then answered, "Yes." Nothing else. The reporter tried another and the answer was, "No." Nothing else. He tried another and another, and the answers were simply "yes" or "no." No explanation from Mellon. Then the reporter was stumped. He left with practically nothing.

One of the things I've always done, and have told others to do, is to brush up on the person they are going to interview. Learn all you can about that person, his hobbies, his prides, his family, his accomplishments. If you're loaded with enough of this, you can carry on a pretty good conversation and work in some of your questions, generally with good results. But the first trick is to get the guy talking. Once he's in that mood—and you get him that way by talking about things that aren't really business—he's off guard a bit and will say things he wouldn't say otherwise. Here's a case in point.

Kap Monohan, our drama critic, was working in Denver at the time Clara Bow was the "It" girl of the films. There was a rumor around that she was going to quit—at the height of her popularity—to marry and have a family. Of course the studio denied it. But Kap reasoned there must be a little fire when there was so much smoke, so when a Denver organization booked the head of Clara's studio for a dinner speech, Kap loaded his guns. He found out everything he could about the man, discovered he was very fond of a couple of little granddaughters—call them Pattie and Connie. He was also proud of his fine home, a swimming pool, and whatnot. He had produced some marvelous movie successes and made some wonderful talent discoveries, such as Clara.

When the man came to town, Kap asked for a private interview, rather than one of those group affairs. It was granted and Kap went to the movie mogul's room. First thing he said, when they shook hands, was: "How are Pattie and Connie?" The Mogul's face brightened, and they went on from there, talking about his home, swimming pool, etc. Then Kap mentioned the many stars this man had discovered. He named them, but purposely left Clara Bow out. "You forgot Clara Bow," the man said. "Oh, yes, I did," Kap said casually. One word and another about her and the movie mogul said: "You've heard about her retiring, I guess?" Kap said: "Oh, yes, but that's a lot of hooey—press agent stuff." Then he started to talk about something else, but the producer insisted on talking about Bow. Kap eventually made like the hell with Clara and the retirement stories. Whereupon the producer got himself all worked up, thus: "If you think she's not quitting, you're crazy. She is." Then he went on to tell him where, when, and how, with details about the home she and her intended were planning, their honeymoon, and whatnot. Kap almost broke a leg getting back to the office and had a world beat. He had used his knowledge of the man, along with a bit of flattery, to get his story. And he never asked a question about Bow. The man told him everything.

Sometimes it is necessary to be brutal. I recall a case some years ago where a man was found dead in a hotel. He was prominent, but there was no obvious reason for suicide. Members of the family wouldn't talk. I finally collared a son who was being a clam, too, for a while. I tried everything, then finally started asking questions that created some suspicion in his mind. Finally he said, "What are you driving at?" I answered: "This. I think he was unhappy at home, had a girl friend, and couldn't take it when she turned him down." That cracked the boy and he told the real story. The man was ill, had been for some time, figured he couldn't be cured. It wasn't so much, but it at least solved the thing.

You can sometimes make a person talk by making him angry. I'm thinking of a big police official who was denying an attempt had been made to bomb the home of an industrial tycoon. The reporter couldn't get anywhere in his interview, so he finally said: "Well, I don't know why I even came here to talk with you. An amateur cop never knows anything and never finds out anything." That did it. The police official shouted: "Amateur cop, huh? Well, listen to this. We've got the fellow who did it in a cell right now."

I knew of another case where a girl reporter made a reticent woman talk because she knew this woman's hobby was collecting Wedgwood china.

Flattery is a great weapon always. Knowledge of your man and his everyday life is another. Ridicule helps in certain cases. But in the long run it's being able to sit down and carry on a casual conversation with your subject that counts.

"Methods depend upon circumstances"

BASCOM TIMMONS, correspondent,
Washington, D. C.

In my forty-six years as an active newspaperman I have talked to many thousands of persons who were on the opposite end of a news story. My purpose has been to elicit information, and the methods depend upon the circumstances.

"Interview without notes"

GLORIA BIGGS, fashion editor,
Hollywood Citizen-News

Interview without taking notes. The two chief advantages of this are that the person being quizzed usually feels much more relaxed and at ease and, in my experience, is more likely to express himself freely; and that the flow of conversation is not halted while the reporter makes hasty notes. Obviously the danger lies in forgetting facts or misstating them in the story. But I have found that the challenge to the memory, which this kind of interviewing offers, produces increased alertness and retention of what the person has said.

For safety's sake, it is usually desirable to make notes of numbers, correct spelling of proper names, dates, and direct quotes. This, I always do. It is surprising, however, how sturdy memory is when it is forced to depend on itself, and not on notes.

"Listening is the key"

ROBERT M. WHITE, II, general manager,
The Mexico (Mo.) *Ledger*

The object of the special interview is to hear enough to tell the other man's story with his words, emotions, and convictions.

157

Keys to Successful Interviewing

My technique is simple. I first ground myself in the man and the subject I'm going to interview him on, then I see him and casually take what notes I must on routine questions which are primarily to get him off the defensive, and then I pocket my pencil and pad and let him talk.

Listening, I believe, is the key to interviewing, providing you know what you're after—your target—and are able to steer the interviewee back to the target from time to time.

Then, if necessary, I get out my pad, at the end of the interview, and review with him a few of the details that I want to be doubly sure of. The remainder of the piece is written from memory. Again, listening is the key to interviewing.

The above technique is sound for the volunteer interviewee. However, some people are determined not to be interviewed.

I got an interview from General Eisenhower—the only one he gave on his trip from Kansas to Europe when he took over NATO—by letting him tell me that he would not give out an interview and then answering: "I understand, sir. I have only one question: What is your advice to young men today?"

That question was a direct shot at a great heart. He couldn't keep from answering, even though he had made up his mind that he would not let anyone have an "interview."

So the question itself can be important in prying open an interview.

And, lastly, too many reporters in my opinion, bypass a real story by being told "no" and not making a story out of that fact.

"Be at ease yourself"

DR. BENJAMIN FINE, education editor,
The New York Times

158

The best reporters are those who, themselves, are at ease and know how to put the person they are interviewing at ease, too. You can frequently get a reticent person to talk by being informal and gradually working up to the main topic you have in mind. I've found the best techniques to be preparing a list of questions in advance—questions which touch the critical issues you want covered during the course of the interview. I feel that the reporter should not hesitate to take ample notes. If this is done, the person being interviewed will recognize that what he said is going to be used and that there is less chance of inaccuracies when the interview appears in print.

"Ask the right questions"

PETER EDSON, Newspaper Enterprise
Association (NEA), Washington, D. C.

The main point, I think, is in the technique of asking questions. Too many reporters ask long and involved questions. They do this because they have not prepared for the interview carefully enough to be able to ask intelligent questions. Being able to ask the right questions, phrasing them simply, and making them short is the easiest way to get direct answers. This applies when the person being interviewed is intelligent and willing to give information. A penetrating question that goes right to the heart of an issue gets a lot better results than a lot of vague questions that skirt around the edges.

But sometimes, when a person being interviewed doesn't want to "give," a deliberately dumb question will get results that a good question won't achieve. It makes the person being interviewed think, "This poor dumb cluck of a reporter doesn't know what time it is or what this is all about, so I had better take a lot of pains to make him understand it or he'll get it all wrong." An offer to let the person being interviewed review the copy, or have it read back to him, also helps sometimes.

I have never found that brow-beating anyone made him more willing to talk, though some reporters use the insult technique with good results.

"Relationship which produces recurrent interviews"

JOHN M. HIGHTOWER, The Associated Press, Washington, D. C.

The most profitable relationship between reporter and news source is that which produces recurrent interviews. To be thus continuous and productive, the relationship must be based on respect and fair-dealing on both sides. It also calls for skill on the reporter's part in determining the kind of approach to which an individual informant will respond. Oftentimes a news source unwilling or unable to answer a direct question is entirely ready to disclose information indirectly or to discuss subjects which obliquely penetrate the matter that the reporter is interested in.

A reporter who persists in failing to understand the rules under which a source operates, or the motives which cause him to talk, is not likely to have very much success in establishing a sustained, productive relationship.

As is true of so many things, there are many ingredients of a successful interview which must generally all be present to assure success, but the lack of any one of which may cause a failure. I have in mind such things as agreeable personality, general intelligence, specific knowledge of the subject in hand, ability to record or remember what is said, understanding of the other fellow's point of view, and the writing skill necessary to organize the results into a story or report. These things are so obvious that it seems to me they should be apparent to everybody, and yet it is surprising how often a man turns up for an interview without adequate preparation of the various ingredients needed in that particular case.

Generally, in Washington reporting, newsmen specialize until they know as much about a subject as many of the people they interview and sometimes, in some cases, they know more. This is a great asset in getting at the truth. Where an interviewer lacks knowledge to be gained from experience, he should by all means prepare himself through research, hasty if necessary, with at least basic information about the subject to be discussed and the man to be interviewed before he keeps his appointment.

"*Get point of view of the subject*"

DELBERT WILLIS, state editor,
The Fort Worth Press

1. Get the point of view of the subject. This does not mean that you must agree with him. But understand his position and let him know that you appreciate his plight. Nodding your head as he talks does not mean you think he is right. It means that you understand what he is talking about. Getting the subject's point of view is the best way to start the natural flow of conversation—a prerequisite to a good interview.

2. Use teaser bait adroitly. If you already have some information, throw it out subtly. The subject might get the impression that you have more information than you really have. If he *thinks* that you already have most of the information, there is no reason why he should hold back the data that he controls.

3. Press home the point that you want the subject's side of the story. In a two-sided controversy, play one side against the other to worm out all the facts. Feed the subject just what information you want him to know about what the other side is doing. Do a little horse trading on information. If you have some facts that the subject is anxious to learn,

trade him facts for facts. But be careful not to violate any confidences in doing this.

4. Beware of "off the record" approaches by a newspaper-wise subject. This is a good way to tie the hands of a cub reporter and he will end up with no story. Try to get everything on the record. If this is not possible, strike a compromise—this is off the record, this is not. But be sure there is complete understanding as to what information is printable. Use the "off the record" material to develop later leads *without* violating his confidence.

5. Don't be overly aggressive on the one hand or timid on the other. Be humble but confident in your manner. Show respect, but expect respect in return.

"Ask meaningful questions"

FRANK DENNIS, managing editor,
Washington (D. C.) *Post*

1. When time permits, study the subject and the interviewee to be able to ask reasonable, intelligent, meaningful questions.

2. Put the first question on some matter of current interest that the interviewee is known to know something about and go on from there.

"Know your subject"

RAYMOND P. BRANDT, Washington Correspondent,
St. Louis Post-Dispatch

The best approach for an interviewer is to know as much about the subject as the interviewee.

"Report how he means it"

KEVIN R. WALLACE, *San Francisco*
(Cal.) *Chronicle*

I try to make out exactly what my victim really wants to say, try to take down quotes accurately as to each idiosyncratic detail so that I can let him report not only what he means but how he means it. Naturally, these quotes come from whatever kind of conversation he and I find congenial in the circumstances of the interview. This is all harder work than it sounds.

"Be selective in material"

HOMER R. CROY, novelist and writer

Because I am interested in biographies at the moment (now doing one on Will Rogers), my interview methods are more tedious and expensive than methods followed by some other writers.

It's hard to sit through two or three versions of an event because people don't see it in the same way. And there's that shadowland where you don't know what is fact and what is imagination. My job is a matter of selection or I would get something as long as the Congressional Record.

"Write what you see and feel"

JIM G. LUCAS, Scripps-Howard Newspaper
Alliance, Washington, D. C.

I've thought much about the questions you raise. I'm disappointed, however, that you limit them to interviewing. In my books, reporting and writing go together. They have been too long separated, and I don't like the degree of specialization. A good reporter who can't present his story is wasting himself needlessly. And a good writer who can't support his story with facts is a phony.

My editor told me when I came to Washington: "There are two ways of getting news in this town. You kick it out of them. Or you charm it out of them. I can't tell you which you should do. You've got to know yourself first. Take your time. Decide. Are you a kicker or a charmer?"

I'm neither a kicker nor a charmer. But—since I must make a choice—I *try* to charm. Co-operate is a better word. My main effort—unless the guy I'm interviewing is out and out ——— —is to convince him I'm basically on his side, without sacrificing any degree of personal integrity. I try to show him I want to be fair. That my story will be objective and honest. I like people too much to be a professional kicker. I confess I sometimes admire those boys who can. But if I try bullying tactics, I usually wind up apologizing.

There are those who can. Andy Tully, a Shanty Irishman on our staff, employs that technique. Andy regards his interviewee as his natural enemy. He may be a nice guy. He may be someone with whom Andy is having drinks later. But Andy assumes—automatically and *per se*—that the guy has something to hide, that any answer he gets will be evasive. In a word—he gives him hell.

As far as I can determine, we both arrive at the same results.

Marshall McNeill of our staff once described me as a reporter with a "deceptively mild and innocent approach." It's not consciously deceptive. I'm basically mild. But—after eighteen years in this business—I don't think I am naïve. I can spot a phony a mile away. When that happens, I let him have it. If I've learned anything in this game, it's integrity. No reporter can last long without it. Having had it forced on him—whether it was there when he started or not—he comes to expect it from everyone else.

Let me cite something that happened in Tokyo:

I'd been trying to learn what was done for Korean rehabilitation. I knew money had been appropriated. But—having spent weary weeks and months in Korea—I saw no results. My investigation led me to believe a certain agency —I won't name it—was boondoggling.

I contacted General X by telephone.

"General," I said, "you have a splendid organization [knowing damn well he didn't] which is doing a particularly splendid job. [An outright lie]. You haven't gotten the credit you deserve. I'd like to do an article about it."

"Ah-hem, Mr. Lucas," said General X, "I make it a policy never to issue statements to the press."

"That's interesting," I replied. "I'm not asking for a statement. I want to do a story about results. Perhaps you have some reports I can read. That should suffice."

"Mr. Lucas," General X got testy. "I've already told you my policy. I'm a busy man." [It was 3:00 P.M. and he'd just gotten in from "lunch."]

"General," I said sweetly, "you've been very kind. You have told your policy without my asking. Now, if you have a moment, let me tell you mine. Whenever I meet a public official spending public funds who takes your attitude, I make it a policy *automatically* to assume he's either an incompetent or an embezzler. And I'm right nine times out of ten."

We both hung up together. I'll treasure that always as the *one* time I thought of the right thing to say at the right time, not later.

Failure to exploit stories is the press' greatest sin. Too many reporters believe they don't need to write—only report. They're sloppy. They're lazy. They're in a rut. I try to learn something every day. Every piece a man turns out should be better—better organized, better written, better presented—than the last.

I spent eighteen months in Korea. Sometimes I cringed when I saw how some men butchered facts they'd risked their lives to get. Too many reporters, I'm convinced, think it's sissy—I use that for want of a better word—to dramatize their story. They glory in being hacks and information gatherers. Poppycock. Before you get readers, you must attract them. And you don't attract them unless you can write.

How do you get a reticent person to talk?

It's a question of gaining his confidence. Let him know you're fair and honest. Let him know you only want to get the facts and present them objectively. You don't need to be servile. But you do need to be sympathetic. You don't win his confidence in one interview. The single-shotter is the bane of a working reporter's existence. He hits and runs. See your man frequently. Meet him socially. Like him if you can. Know something about him and his interest. Talk to him about something else—yesterday's disastrous ball game if you're a Senator fan (and I'm one of those hapless derelicts).

I cite two examples.

a. Several years ago, I did a piece about the army-navy feud in which the Gallery Report (written by Rear Admiral Dan V. Gallery) was featured. I did not treat it gently. Later, I asked to see Admiral Gallery. He was—he told me later—"scared spitless." He didn't know me. He was afraid of me. He saw me—but reluctantly. I wrote nothing out of that first interview. We simply chatted; got acquainted. We found we had mutual friends. Later, I ran across him in a coffee bar. We flipped to see who'd pay. Today, we're very close friends. We both believe in the other.

b. Some time back, I was tipped off that Archibald Alexander was to be named assistant army secretary. I knew nothing about him except that he'd run for the Senate on the Democratic ticket in New Jersey. I assumed—always dangerous—that any New Jersey Democrat was a Hague man. Our papers the next day had a clean scoop—"Hague Lieutenant Gets Pentagon Post." It was correct in every detail save one—Archie was the leader of the *anti-Hague* Democrats of New Jersey.

My next column was an abject apology. I asked to meet him and apologized personally. Archie has been a personal friend since.

As for techniques, I don't know. I went to Korea in July, 1950, for a two-month tour. I stayed until Christmas Eve, 1951. I began writing and it started clicking. Don't ask me how or why.

At one time, my editors sent a man over to help—and perhaps replace me.

"Give him the formula," they cabled.

That stumped me. I didn't know—still don't. I don't even know I have one. I have no hard and fast rules. But if I have a formula, it's this:

I write what I see and what I feel, I stress "feel." I try to write what I sense should be written. I try to drain every last ounce of drama—yes, drama—out of every fact I present. That doesn't mean over-writing. I try not to. I like short sentences. You can pack a wallop in a few words. If you want to. If you try.

8

Now, If You Ask Me

ALWAYS REMEMBER that you must be able to distinguish between newsy facts and those of little or no news value. This requires exercise of that "sixth sense," often called the "nose for news." Without this ability, you have no sense of direction in your interviewing. A knowledge and appreciation of news values help you solve two distinct problems in every assignment: first, to recognize the news value of the story itself; and secondly, to select the elements of greatest interest. If you are on top of the story, you will recognize clues which may be very casual but which may lead to the discovery of important news.

Good copy doesn't just happen—it doesn't just flow —it is usually the result of a reporter's being "on his toes." Your interviewee is usually lacking in a sense of news values. That is why he is seldom moved by the reporter's threadbare question, "Any news today?" It is the reporter's task to know enough about his source to ask intelligent questions. You can't go in "cold" and get a "hot" story.

The important way in which the ace interviewer differs from the run-of-the-mine reporter is an unusual flexibility and adaptability, a capacity for seeing drama in the commonplace, and a tolerance for the ideas of others. He

knows what to do and when to do it. A city editor described
his best interviewer as a "slick, well-balanced guy who seldom zigs when he ought to zag."

You need not have a gift of gab to succeed as an
interviewer. Maybe you are shy. So was the late Ernie Pyle,
who became a much-loved correspondent in World War II
because of his treatment of G. I. Joe. In an article, "The
Hoosier Letter-Writer," in the *Saturday Evening Post*, Frederick C. Painton wrote of him: "Everywhere he went, soldiers waved them [his columns] under his nose. He came to
know a thousand soldiers by name, thousands more by sight.
Overnight, as it were, the skinny guy of the column has become known to millions of Americans. As the cheerful, droll
character in the column he has lived in foxholes with the ad-
vanced infantry, with the gunners of the big 155's, in the
desert with bomber commands, swapped gossip with soldiers
from one end of North Africa to the other. Always Ernie
Pyle, the Midwest farm boy, darting around a battlefield
like a curious bird. That's the character you meet in the
column.

"Actually, the real Ernie Pyle is not that gregarious,
easy-talking character at all. He is a shy, extremely sensitive
man of forty-three, who has been tortured for years by acute
self-consciousness. He likes people enormously, but he is so
timid that the prospect of meeting just one sets his heart to
pounding. 'I suffer agony in anticipation of meeting anybody, for fear they won't like me,' he says. 'Once I'm past
the meeting I'm all right.' He is very quiet and seldom says
much."

Stuck away somewhere in every interview is a central idea. That idea must be found, must be timed, must be
tuned, to the public pulse. Else—you have what? A jumble
of words—dead, flabby words. What's more, you must dig
out the idea, dramatize it, and know exactly how much your
readers would like to know about it.

You are anxious to play up the interviewee's most startling remark. Suppose you have interviewed Mr. J., who has just returned from Korea. For fourteen of the fifteen minutes you conversed, Mr. J. said nothing which would make copy. Then in a brief aside he remarked, "Our army officers live in luxury while the fighting men lack some of the necessities of life." Now there is a startling declaration and is lead material. If you use it, explain that it was an incidental remark. If not, readers will imagine that his whole interview was a blast at the differences in the ways of life of the men in service. By pulling a side remark out of the original context, the reporter may give the wrong impression. It is better to play up the speaker's attitude toward his subject as a whole.

Your creative imagination will really get a workout when you are traveling with a candidate for political office with the assignment of doing a daily story. The candidate will probably give the same speech day after day. Here are two suggestions: (1) Listen to (or obtain after the speech) his comments on affairs of interest in the particular community, and (2) seek comments from leaders and other citizens on their reactions to his speech. Always stick around, because the speaker may leave his daily memorized message and utter a "quotable quote."

Then there was the reporter who asked the young lady who showed up at the blood-donor station in Texas, "Do you know your type?" "Oh, yes," came the confident reply, "I'm the sultry type."

You must respect release dates when information or stories are given you in advance. In this category you will find copies of speeches, official reports, and certain statements. To "jump" a release date is dangerous from several standpoints. There may be important changes in the news after it is prepared in advance, or something might happen to cause the anticipated news to fail to materialize. A speaker, for instance, may die or become too ill to appear. This same principle applies to less important stories. If you break a release date and run a story on any event which has not occurred, you may offend the informant or the organization or institution. Frederick S. Siebert in *The Rights and Privileges of the Press* declared that common-law rights to a story submitted to a single newspaper belong to the originator of that story up to the time of publication.

A reporter can no longer claim "exclusive rights" to a story originating from a query when broad national interest is involved. Routine or feature matter is covered by a limited right, but not when the story is of paramount interest to the nation, it has been explained by Andrew Berding, director of information of the United States Department of Defense. In case of the minor story or feature, which does not involve security or is not of great importance, the correspondent is given guaranteed exclusivity. "To my mind," Berding explained, "there are no 'exclusive property rights' in the news of a development which perhaps has involved millions of dollars of the taxpayers' money and thousands of engineering hours." If the story is important and does not threaten public security, then it is released to all media.

Some writers no longer rely on the one-shot interview when doing a personality profile. Maurice Zolotow, who has written more than 120 biographical sketches for the *Saturday Evening Post, Cosmopolitan, Collier's, The Reader's Digest,* and other magazines, stays with his subject for several weeks. Describing his techniques in *Writer's Digest,* he says: ". . . most people in public life are used to being interviewed by newspaper reporters rushed for time and are compelled to ask questions and get answers bearing on a few specific points." He grants that the writer must have the facts of a person's life. "But the personality-piece writer," he continues, "has to dig underneath the facts." Zolotow believes that frequently a person's real character is concealed by a public mask, built up for many years as a result of dozens of interviews at which the subject automatically has given his prepared set of answers.

In his practice of catching his subject in real life situations, Zolotow has had many interesting experiences. "I have watched Ray Bolger get massaged, Tallulah Bankhead disrobe to the bare skin, Ethel Merman fire a governess for her children. I have argued against vegetarianism with Fred Allen (a food faddist) and against Christian Science with Paul Hartman, the dancer, a devout Scientist."

Dictating machines are replacing the reporter's traditional pad and pencil in important interviewing situations. Hilliard Schendorf, Associated Press radio writer, New York City, got the idea of using a direct recording when he was assigned to do a series of interviews that were to be used verbatim. It worked out better than expected.

He explained it in *Editor and Publisher:*

"If you have to take notes at an interview, whether you realize it or not you can only do one thing at a time. You either think and listen or stop and write. It's like the old Mississippi steamboat that had only enough power to either blow the whistle or turn the paddle wheels—it couldn't do both. If you can't control the interview, as at a news conference, you miss something or must ask to have an answer repeated.

"If you can control the interview you stop while you write, and these pauses cause some people to lose their trend of thought. And they certainly discourage them from volunteering the spontaneous extra things that sometimes make a good deal of difference. A person will say a lot more if he's not interrupted, especially when speaking on something in which he is deeply interested.

"Not many reporters make altogether complete notes in doing an interview. The tendency is to pick out the trend of the story that looks promising. Sometimes you find that what didn't appear worth putting down at the beginning becomes essential toward the end. That means more backtracking if you're to get the thing complete, unless you have a transcript of the entire conference."

In addition, the small recorder saves time. Mr. Schendorf first used the machine in interviewing Dr. John Harley, head of the atomic warning system in the United States. And the feature writer explained later, "I got material in twenty-five minutes that would have taken me an hour or more to get had I had to take longhand notes."

Objectivity in reporting may be carried too far. In fact, it may become a false god, Gideon Seymour, executive editor of the *Minneapolis Star* and *Tribune*, told a Sigma Delta Chi audience in Chicago. Objectivity has become in too many instances "a kind of laziness, an evasion rather than a meeting of journalistic responsibility." He quoted the late Raymond Clapper as saying, "We commonly make two mistakes about people: we underestimate their intelligence and we overestimate the amount of information they have."

Few terms are more widely used or abused than "off the record." Even veteran Washington correspondents, who bump up against the term most often, have trouble agreeing on exactly what it means.

In all probability it originates in courtroom procedure, where the judge may instruct the court stenographer not to record certain testimony or discussion. H. L. Mencken credits New York's Governor Al ("Let's look at the record") Smith for bringing it into wider use. It became popular in Washington during the New Deal.

In Washington, politicians often use "off the record" when what they really mean is, "Don't quote me" (i.e., do not attribute this statement to me). Newsmen declare that talking straight has become a lost art in Washington, and that they have to fight their way through a semantic jungle. Since "off the record" has become both confused and useless, the only course for good newsmen is to pin their sources down as to what use may be made of the material. If the sources really want it suppressed, for no good reason, most good newsmen refuse to accept the terms and go digging for facts elsewhere.

Former President Harry S. Truman once gave a speech that was billed as "off the record" before the Women's Press Club; yet it was televised. Even publishers bumble the term. One newsman recalls that during World War II, *Look's* publisher, Gardner Cowles, told a radio audience that he was going to let them in on some "off-the-record" stuff. The Overseas Press Club published a collection of some of its members' most memorable experiences; its title: *Off The Record.*

Do you like people? Do they fascinate you? "I never met a man I didn't like," said Will Rogers. Now undoubtedly, the cowboy-humorist met bores, pests, and cheats just as the rest of us do. Friends asked him, "How could you possibly like everybody?" Then he explained, "Of course I don't approve of all the things that people do, but there is some goodness and some cussedness in all of us. If you know a man well enough, you can always find something interesting about him. It is just a matter of what you are looking for." The biggest compliment you can pay a human being is to like him. That's the belief of Elmer Wheeler, specialist in the word magic of salesmanship. As he explains it, "It does something to us inside to know that someone likes us. It makes us feel good. It inflates our ego. It makes us feel important— and it touches our heart. Instinctively we like a person who likes us."

Often a celebrity is publicity conscious and will work out special phrases for speeches and interviews. In the case of Winston Churchill, "often what appears a spontaneous piece of fun has been carefully rehearsed," Alastair Forbes, well-known British writer and long-time friend of the Churchill family, reveals.

A reporter faces a variety of temptations. One of these is to become a personal publicity agent for an influential person. Some public officials and other important personages use flattery and other means to gain undue influence with newsmen or throw their favorites an occasional exclusive story. Listen to this warning from Frank S. Adams of the *New York Times:* "But the reporter who falls for these devices always discovers that there is a *quid pro quo;* that he is expected to float trial balloons, which his source can disavow if the public reaction is unfavorable; or that he must give his 'friend' something more than a fair break in controversial stories."

Some persons, many of them important, may try to intimidate you to get better coverage of their activities and views. They may tell your editor that you are unfair. Fortunately, most news executives will back up their reporters when criticism comes. On other occasions, your detractors will pitch your rival a good exclusive. How can you meet these forms of attack? The best defense is to develop a reputation for integrity, trustworthiness, and fairness.

Paste this proverb in your hat: "The fool tries to convince me with his reasons; the wise man persuades with my own."

Although the court has the right to exclude newspapermen and to control its records, it cannot curtail the press from printing accurate accounts obtained from other sources. This principle has been established legally in several states. Reporters may not attend sessions of a grand jury and should not attempt to question grand jurors, who are under oath to maintain secrecy. Newsmen may question witnesses and attorneys. In no circumstances should the press publish stories which reveal the status of a jury's deliberations. Often a reporter will obtain the verdict from the jurors as they leave the jury room to make their report in order to give the public immediate news of the verdict. Sometimes the reporter will tell his readers how long a time was required for the jury to reach a verdict. But the reporter should be present when the verdict is read. In this way he not only learns the verdict but can witness its effect upon the principals, and he may obtain statements from the attorneys and the principals. The effect of the verdict upon the principals and the spectators will usually make a strong human-interest story.

Oftentimes you will find it difficult to pin a person down for serious information. A young lady correspondent once asked Henry Morgan, radio comedian, about his hobbies. "Flying and tropical fish," he replied. Delighted, she ventured, "What kind of tropical fish?" "The live ones," Morgan told her, and, when she began to look confused, he explained that he gave the dead ones to a mouse named Gabriel.

Your attitude toward the interviewee is subject to changes. As a matter of fact, you are constantly making assumptions at each stage in each interview. These are subject to change as you develop new insight and understanding of the person with whom you are talking. And if you aren't extremely careful, your interpretation is likely to be founded not on the actual situation but on factors you have contributed to the experience. Theodore Reik calls the psychoanalyst's faculty of sensing the meaning of what be observes "listening with the third ear." He explains that this process begins on the conscious levels of intelligence, is integrated with previous knowledge and emotions in the unconscious, and is brought into consciousness after it has been transmuted into a meaningful and useful interpretation of what the subject has revealed.

News from hospitals sometimes presents a problem for reporters. Hospitals have strict rules that protect the privacy of their patients. In all except rare instances, a reporter can usually get the name and address of the patient, the character of the illness or injury, and perhaps the name of the attending physician. Often the physician will give additional information, at times requesting that his name not be used in the story. As in almost any other news situation, the response of your source may be determined very strongly by your previous relationships. Where you must go in "cold," specific knowledge of hospital administration patterns can come to your aid. In some instances, you must obtain most of the information from sources other than the hospital. In cases of accidents or homicides, the police obtain and report the names of all available witnesses, whom you can interview.

Never forget this fact: As an interviewer, you are an interpreter. Unless you are extremely careful, you are likely to take the jargon of professional experts and repeat it verbatim in your finished story. Robert Gunning spoke accurately when he stated in *The Technique of Clear Writing*, "If his job is to be done right, a reporter must be a good translator." If the diplomat discusses a "bilateral concordat," the newsman should let his readers know that the document in question is a "two-way pact." When an official predicts that a "jurisdictional strike" may take place, the reporter should define that term. He should point out that this means that a strike may take place if the members of one union refuse to work when those of another union are employed.

177

Howard W. Blakeslee, Associated Press science editor from 1928 until his death in 1952, had the knack of making science news interesting while keeping it accurate. As an interviewer, he was tops. He took special pleasure in needling scientists when their briefing seemed vague. His whole approach: Take the wind out of the windbags. Younger members of the staff asked Mr. Blakeslee shortly before his death how they could have half of his "go-get-'em" when and if they reached seventy-two. "The secret," said H. W. B., "is never stop being a reporter."

Even after you have obtained facts from the respondent, you still have the problem of determining what the facts are. Your situation is similar to that of the social case worker and the lawyer. Mary E. Richmond, in her book, *Social Diagnosis,* applied the fact-finding in social work after studying the law of evidence as evolved from the long experience of the legal profession. She distinguishes the types of evidence, following the classifications of real, testimonial, circumstantial, and hearsay. She found that the competence of the interviewee depends partly on his capacities of attention and memory and on his susceptibility to suggestion and questions. She also discovered that the bias of the person may be racial, national, environmental, or simply that of self-interest.

Watch for bits of wisdom in your interviews. One afternoon, for instance, Sir Wilmott Lewis, well-known Washington correspondent of the *London Times,* encountered Charles Evans Hughes and congratulated him on his hearty appearance. "Thank you," said the Justice. "I feel very well, all things considered. I am reminded of Elihu Root's remark when he was eighty and I complimented him on his good health: 'Yes, I am just about as good as I ever was—for one hour a day.'"

Reporters must improve their interviewing skills if newspapers hope to compete with television. Just before the Republican Convention in Chicago in 1952, Dick Thornburg, Scripps-Howard's news executive, urged in a memo to his staff: "Our job more than at any time in the past will be to provide interpretive material. Why did Joe Blow make that kind of speech? What influence did it have? What votes did it change? Also, forward-looking stories telling the readers what to expect that evening on TV . . . telling what happened in the back rooms and caucuses the TV viewer did not see."

Sometimes your questions yield amusing answers. A reporter for a California newspaper asked an eighty-five-year-old man, "To what do you attribute your longevity?" The old fellow answered, "I don't know yet. I'm still dickering with two breakfast food companies."

Don't expect to attain perfection in judging your interviewees. Naturally, your personal judgment influences your reaction to the other person. And here's something else: Never forget that a certain trait may be strong in one situation and hardly noticeable in another. If you dress conservatively, then you are very likely to say that the conservatively dressed interviewee presents a good appearance. Since all persons differ widely in ability to appraise obvious traits such as personal appearance, how much greater must be the divergence of estimates of subtle qualities such as courage, truthfulness, sincerity, and emotional stability.

Sooner or later you will be caught in a situation in which the interviewee asks you a question you may want to answer only to yourself. When Carl Victor Little, triple-threat man (book reviewer, columnist, and chief of the editorial page) of the *Houston Press*, was a young reporter, he went into a hotel suite to interview William Jennings Bryan.

The subject was Bryan's opposition to teaching evolution, it is reported in *Scripps-Howard News.* Bryan entered the room clad only in BVD's. His legs, arms, and chest were masses of black hairs. He paced the room as he talked and finally, striking a pose, struck his chest with both fists and exclaimed dramatically: "Monkeys! Man descended from monkeys! Look at me. Do I look like a monkey?" In Little's notes on the interview was a tiny scribble, "Yes."

When you find a person who is flexible-minded about many things, do not be surprised when he clamps his mind shut in a certain area. Suppose, for instance, that he sees nothing but evil in college sports. It is useless to argue with him or try to explain. His reaction is final. His mind is set. Even though he is open to suggestion and may welcome new evidence on other topics, he is fixed in his attitude toward college athletics. Psychologists say that such a case represents an "area rigidity." Can you explain such behavior? Only by delving deep into his emotional past— usually much deeper than your interviewee can go himself—could you help in explaining his special vulnerability.

Many persons of prominence will evade questions and even lie to newspapermen. They may send word by their secretaries that they are out of the city when they are at their desks. In fact, often a newsworthy person may deny any knowledge of a story which the reporter has proof that he knows everything about. They may go even further, Curtis D. MacDougall reminds us in *Newsroom Problems and Policies:* "They may assume disguises, sneak down rear stairways, and even leave the city, state, or country to avoid meeting both the press and the law." Just what right the press should grant such persons to control news concerning themselves or to what extent subterfuge is justifiable in dealing with them is a difficult question to answer. You and your editor must decide: Is this incident in the public interest? Your answer to that question will determine future action.

Sooner or later you are likely to be caught in the cross-fire of organizations or groups. Even the smallest and mildest groups often engage in petty battles and disputes. You must resist your natural desire to "take sides" on many occasions. John Paul Jones warns that "many of the battles are just ships that pass in the night and the reporter who jumps on one side may soon find himself disliked by both sides when members of the 'teams' shift." Wise is the newsman who remains on the outside and refuses to carry tales back and forth between the opposing groups.

The next edition is always urging you to hurry. You are doing an interviewing assignment. You want to get meaning from the interviewee's words—meaning which will tie in with what the reader knows or needs to know. This can't be just a hit-and-run treatment. You must serve it up so that you catch the full significance of the event. After press time you may often ask yourself, "Should I become a specialist in one area or subject?" Louis M. Lyons, curator of the Nieman Fellowships, doesn't think so. He insists that any good staff reporter at a given time on a given assignment has to become a specialist *pro tem.* In a talk before the California Editors' Conference, Lyons stated that a good staff reporter "has to be a specialist in one issue this month and in another next month. He has to be a versatile specialist—capable of absorbing all the facts fast, of understanding and relating all the facts, fast—but still he has an outside look at them all." Even though the reporter is specializing more and more, he keeps his amateur standing. He can interpret the experts so that the reader will read and understand.

As an interviewing practitioner, you must avoid trite phrases and bromides. You have admired the way Bob

181

Considine can make words sing. Does he just sit at the typewriter and allow inspiration from on high to flow through his fingers? Not exactly. Like many another talented newsman, he has a system of jotting down ideas. Whenever an idea or phrase comes to him—riding home, shaving in the morning, or watching a baseball game—he writes it in his little black notebook. When an occasion comes to use one, he uses it—and then crosses it off. W. Somerset Maugham's idea notebooks occupy fifteen thick volumes and cover a period of fifty-eight years. If you are to grow creatively, you must be alert to fresh phrases, clever expressions, and words that sparkle, and then you must record them for future use.

You have a definite personality. It belongs to you. You want to make the most of the personality which Providence has provided. You have set up the specific goal of strengthening your abilities as an interviewer. The first step is one of honest self-analysis. Do a little private bookkeeping. In one column, without excuse or timidity, set down your weaknesses. Are you conceited? Pessimistic? Untidy? Complaining? Careless? Unreliable? Lazy? Self-centered?—and so on down the line. In another column, list your virtues. Cheerful? Friendly? Understanding? Enthusiastic? Reliable? Poised? Accurate? Then, as Dr. Albert Wiggam puts it, "Begin here—and keep at it for the next fifty years."

Covering the police station creates special problems for the reporter. He must certainly use discretion, for instance, in accepting the version of either the police or the accused person. Chilton R. Bush, in *Newspaper Reporting of Public Affairs*, states his belief that the reporter "should treat the so-called confession of the defendants made to police officials and prosecuting attorneys in light of the local practices of the police in obtaining signed confessions." Be wary of confessions that may have been obtained by inhumane methods. Always handle crime news with restraint.

There were no interviewers in Rochefoucauld's day. Yet his apt warning is just as true today: "The desire of appearing clever often prevents our becoming so."

Words are powerful. That is why what you put between quotation marks and attribute to the interviewee should be accurate. *The Buffalo* (N. Y.) *Evening News* urges its reporters to get quotations "with precise accuracy." Say the editors, "We have no right or wish to take liberties with the words we attribute to another within quotation marks."

What about handouts? As a general rule, the mimeographed or typed statement usually presents the person or institution publicized in the most favorable light. Accept the handout as a tip for a story. And then go back to the news source and ask enough questions to make the story complete. Obviously, the type of handout you receive will depend upon the past reliability of the source, the objectivity of the publicity writer, the purpose of the story, and other variables. Here is a good test: An ethical publicist is always happy to get additional material, steer you to persons who can answer your questions, and assist in other ways even when you are on the trail of a story which may be unfavorable to his organization.

Occasionally someone will complain because you wrote a story which did not give his side of the situation. You may explain that you tried to reach him and failed and that you did write that he "was not available for comment" in the story. But that doesn't satisfy him. Then explain that you will be glad to get his statement and use it as another story.

Once there was a reporter who could write well and knew his news values. Seemingly, he had about everything needed to make a top-flight writer. But one thing was wrong.

He spoke in a high-pitched, excited manner. With practice, some flexibility of tone can be developed by most people. You will speak clearly and loudly enough for the listener to hear and enunciate syllables carefully; but in addition to these qualities, you should develop as pleasant a speaking voice as possible. It will help you as an interviewer to develop a voice which registers enthusiasm, calmness, strong convictions, and humor.

How can you improve your voice? Listen to those who speak well and try to imitate the best qualities of their voices. Here is Helen Hayes' advice to some embryonic troupers: "Know your voice. Make a record of it. You may be surprised or horrified. Your voice may be perfect, or may have the rasping sound of chalk on a blackboard. Most important, if you don't like the sound of your voice, do something about it."

Are you hasty in your judgment of others? If so, consider this old prayer which the Omaha Indians taught their young braves: "Great Spirit, help me never to judge another until I have walked two weeks in his moccasins."

Techniques of interviewing can never be listed in ten easy lessons. Every situation has its variables. Edgar Ansel Mowrer, famous correspondent for the *Chicago Daily News,* once told me: "It is completely impossible for me to list any formal techniques for inducing refractory subjects to talk. You might as well try to reduce courtship to a formula. It seems to be true that successful Don Juans do develop certain formulae successfully. But personally, I have never known in advance just how I intended to open a conversation with a person whom I wished to interview. It all depended upon the circumstances and inspiration of the moment. Obviously, I am familiar with what might be called the chief strategic plans; but I do not consider that there would be anything gained by attempting to formalize a form of activity, which, in the last analysis, remains firmly imbedded in the infinite complexity of human relations."

Good interview copy is generally the result of a direct and personal meeting of the minds between an alert writer and a fairly responsive person. If it is filtered through too many intermediaries, no matter how well meaning they may be, it often gets watered down and weakened to the point of dullness.

Some doctors are beginning to lift the curtain of secrecy which surrounds their professional activities. Dr. Eric Oldberg, head of the department of neuro-surgery at the University of Illinois College of Medicine, served as the press observer when the Brodie Siamese twins were separated in a twelve-hour operation in 1952. He briefed reporters at a press conference the day following the operation. Many of the reporters expressed a desire to interview the neurosurgeons, the anesthetist, the pediatricians, and the plastic surgeons. But most of the newsmen were satisfied with the briefing given them by Dr. Oldberg because they realized that doctors and others who assisted wanted to avoid possible violation of the medical code of ethics.

War correspondents face many barriers in their news gathering. The censorship code (which was set up without any advice from members of the press) contains two sections which most correspondents believe to be dangerous. One prohibits publication of anything which might "give aid and comfort" to the enemy, and the other stops any stories which criticize or bring discredit upon any branch of the armed services. Upon his return from Korea, Robert Miller, United Press roving correspondent, pointed out that a newsman soon learns that the military will tolerate no criticism, however constructive, from civilian newsmen. Three-fourths of all Korean news originates directly or indirectly from public information officers of the army, navy, marine and air force offices. The real danger is that a correspondent, unless he is extremely careful, may rely more and more on the P.I.O.'s and their handouts for news instead of going out and digging up his own yarns and checking his own facts.

By putting the golden rule into action, you practice what psychology calls empathy—"the imaginative projection of one's consciousness into another being." Just how much you do this depends upon your interest in others, your intelligence, and the use of your creative imagination.

Most writers dash to their typewriters as soon as possible after an interview. Why? For one thing, the scribbled notes may be harder to read the next day or even an hour or two later. Furthermore, some of the background may be lost if too much time elapses between the time of the conversation and the typing time. Eunice Jones Stickland reports in the *Writer's Digest* that "While my feeling for the interview is keen, I can put into words many impressions which are not found in the notes."

Too many reporters fondly imagine that they could scale the heights as interviewers by imitating successful writers. Up to a certain point, they can. But what the imitator forgets is that the top-flight interviewer has attained a certain distinction. Reputation and acceptance are never awarded to the hack writer, but to the exceptional one—to the reporter who has capitalized upon his unique merits. Develop interviewing distinction—an identity which sets you apart from the mediocrity of the mass—and see how compelling are your attractions.

When all is said and done, the expert interviewer is not the swashbuckling headline-hunter often dreamed up by Hollywood casting directors. Rather, the ace news gatherer has a "nose for news." He makes friends easily. His writing sings. Most important of all, he can get people to talk.

He must know certain rules, basic strategies. But he won't be bound by them. You can't interview by rules or write by them.

But I do insist that in interviewing, just as in any other professional skill, there are certain rules to be learned, although the reason for learning them is not to follow them slavishly. Interviewing is not yet at the point where success comes simply by following rules. Rules, you see, are never absolute. They are tools of the craft, not the craft itself.

Learning them is like learning the rules of grammar. Knowing them does not guarantee that you will become an expert interviewer, any more than a knowledge of grammar assures you of becoming a Steinbeck.

In fact, the ability to break the rules and get away with it is what separates the truly creative interviewer from the hack. To stand above the crowd, he must not only take from, but add to, the accumulated strategies, techniques, and processes of interviewing. He digs beneath the surface and asks questions—questions which bring forth facts essential to an enlightened public opinion. He gets vibrant, fresh color. New angles, different and significant, put a *plus* into his writings.

He is more than a reporter; he is an interpreter of the highest of all arts—the art of living.

Appendix I

Take My Word For It

(Synonyms for "said," as used in newspaper and magazine interview stories)

according to	cited	disclosed
accused	claimed	discussed
acknowledged	commented	divulged
added	complained	elucidated
advanced	conceded	emphasized
advised	concluded	ended
affirmed	confessed	exclaimed
agreed	confided	explained
alleged	confirmed	exploded
announced	contended	exposed
answered	continued	expostulated
approved	countered	expounded
argued	declaimed	expressed
asserted	declared	felt
avowed	decided	found
believed	demanded	foretold
called for	denied	gave notice
cautioned	denoted	held that
certified	described	hinted
charged	designed	imparted

implied	praised	returned
indicated	predicated	revealed
inferred	predicted	reviewed
informed	proclaimed	shouted
insinuated	professed	sighed
insisted	prompted	signified
iterated	pronounced	specified
intimated	propounded	spoke
jested	proposed	stated
lashed	protested	stressed
lauded	put forward	submitted
made public	questioned	suggested
maintained	quoted	summarized
mentioned	recalled	swore
murmured	recapitulated	talked
named	recited	testified
narrated	recounted	thought
noted	reiterated	told
notified	related	trumpeted
observed	remarked	turned
opined	reminded	uncovered
orated	repeated	urged
ordered	replied	uttered
pleaded	reported	viewed
pointed out	responded	voiced
posed	retorted	warned

Appendix II

Greeley Gets the Credit

IF HORACE GREELEY hadn't taken some of his own advice—"Go West, young man, Go West"—in the summer of 1859, he would not have received credit for being the first man to write a newspaper interview in the question-and-answer form. Here is what happened.

Mr. Greeley started overland to California. En route it occurred to him to stop in Utah and get Brigham Young's views on religion and politics. So Greeley paused in Salt Lake City for a two-hour interview with the Mormon leader. Readers of Greeley's *New York Tribune* got an amazingly frank report of Mr. Young's views. The editor used the story as a potent weapon in his assault on those who opposed the rights of women. Only three years later Congress, in response to the pressure Greeley helped generate, outlawed polygamy.

Some historians believe that James Gordon Bennett, editor of the *New York Herald*, was the father of the interview in journalism. The elder Bennett interviewed Martin Van Buren on a visit to Washington in January, 1839. More recently historians have eliminated the Bennett article (which was published January 12, 1839) from consideration as a real interview. They point out that the story is high in subjective impressions and low in information content, and thus is not a true interview.

Greeley's personal interview with Young, head of the Church of Jesus Christ of Latter Day Saints (Mormons), appeared in the *New York Tribune* on August 20, 1859. Although its lead is slow-moving, the article contains information on slavery, Mormonism, and other live topics of the day. George Turnbull, professor of journalism in the University of Oregon, who has made a special study of the history of the interview, credits Greeley as the originator of this phase of journalism.

Look at sections of the 1839 Bennett article. It was sent to the *Herald* as one of a series of letters from the national capital, and occupied a full column. Here are the only quotations:

"How do you do, Mr. Bennett?" said Mr. Van Buren with a half a smile.

To which Mr. Bennett replied: "Pretty well, I thank you," with another half a smile.

Bennett did not use indirect quotations. He did, however, include quite a bit of subjective comment, as the following excerpt indicates:

"When my turn came, I went up to His Excellency. He held out his hand. It was soft and oily. I took hold of it gently, by the very hand, too, which has quizzed him most unmercifully during the last four years, in those annoying four-line paragraphs."

There follows the mutual salutation previously quoted and then: "I looked into his face—his eyes wandered over the carpet, probably thinking at the moment of the meeting of Agamemnon and Achilles. I was almost on the verge of bursting into a horse laugh, at the vagaries of human nature, but being in the presence of the head of the Democratic party, I restrained myself.

"I sat down on the sofa, crossed my legs, and looked very knowingly into the fine hickory fire blazing high—the other gentlemen ranged around."

Then he apparently interviewed President Van Buren, but did not write the interview. What he did write follows:

"Several topics were introduced and briefly discussed—a little on local politics—a little on land speculations—a little on the weather. On land speculations the President perpetrated a sarcasm [which Mr. Bennett kept discreetly to himself], although he seldom deals in that luxury. He then addressed himself to me and afterward to my friend.

"I think I never saw Mr. Van Buren look better and he seems in excellent spirits. He dresses in black throughout, with great neatness and taste, and seems to fill his chair with ease and self-possession. In front of his seat hung a portrait of Bolivar, the same, I believe, which graced the apartment when Old Hickory occupied it.

"After a few minutes he rose and departed, giving room to other visitors.

"What a singular being! Ten years ago I knew Mr. Van Buren as a senator, when he had no more idea of being President than I had. What a remarkable illustration of the free institutions of this land! Forty or fifty years ago, Mr. Van Buren was a poor boy in Kinderhook, unnoticed, unknown and unheralded—now he is President of twenty millions of people and a territory second in size to all Europe. And not only is he President now, but there is a strong presentiment here that he will be re-elected, in spite of all that the Whigs can do. And even that he will name his successor also."

After making this prophecy, Bennett proceeded to give his opinions on the secretary of the treasury. His article, interesting as it was to *Herald* readers, is not an interview in the strict journalistic sense, Professor Turnbull declares.

It is true that Gerrit Smith's interview of twenty years later is an authentic example of what is known as a newspaper interview, but as Professor Turnbull has reminded us, "the fact remains that the Greeley interview had preceded this fine bit of work [the Smith interview] by several months, and that Bennett had every opportunity to see it in the *Tribune.* That he adopted the interview technique so soon afterward, albeit vicariously through his reporter (who, unfortunately, is anonymous), is a credit to his journalistic sense in knowing a good thing when he saw it."

Greeley wrote his interview with Mr. Young in dialogue form under the date of July 13 and dispatched it to the *Tribune* and other papers. Here is the lead, written in the tempo of the times:

> My friend, Dr. Bernhisel, M. C., took me this afternoon by appointment to meet Brigham Young, President of the Mormon Church, who had expressed a willingness to receive me at 2 P.M. We were very cordially welcomed at the door by the President, who led us into the second-story parlor of the largest of his houses (he has three), where I was introduced to Heber C. Kimball, General Wells, General Ferguson, Albert Carrington, Elias Smith, and several other leading men in the church, with two full-grown sons of the President. After some unimportant conversation on general topics, I stated that I had come in quest of fuller knowledge regarding the doctrines and polity of the Mormon church, and would like to ask some questions bearing directly on these, if there were no objection. President Young avowed his willingness to respond to all pertinent inquiries, and the conversation proceeded substantially as follows:

The interview itself starts with the newspaperman's question, followed by the answer of the news source, with each paragraph introduced by the initials of the person speaking, H.G. and B.Y.

Question-and-Answer Style
[It was 1859, and it didn't take Greeley long to get down to the question of the hour.]

> H.G. What is the position of your church with re-
> spect to slavery?
>
> B.Y. We consider it of Divine institution, and not
> to be abolished until the curse pronounced on
> Ham shall have been removed from his de-
> scendants.
>
> H.G. Are any slaves now held in this territory?
>
> B.Y. There are.
>
> H.G. Do your territorial laws uphold slavery?
>
> B.Y. Those laws are printed—you can read for
> yourself. If slaves are brought here by those
> who owned them in the States, we do not
> favor their escape from the service of those
> owners.
>
> H.G. Am I to infer that Utah, if admitted as a mem-
> ber of the Federal Union, will be a slave state?
>
> B.Y. No; she will be a free state. Slavery here
> would prove useless and unprofitable. I re-
> gard it generally as a curse to the master. I
> myself hire many laborers and pay them fair
> wages; I could not afford to own them. I can
> do better than subject myself to an obligation
> to feed and clothe their families, to provide
> and care for them in sickness and health.
> Utah is not adapted to slave labor.

The other topics considered are presented in similar form and style. Then follows the concluding paragraph:

Such is, as nearly as I can recollect, the substance
of nearly two hours of conversation, wherein much
was said incidentally that would not be worth re-

porting, even if I could remember and reproduce it, and wherein others bore a part; but, as President Young is the first minister of the Mormon church, and bore the principal part of the conversation, I have reported his answers alone to my questions and observations. The others appeared uniformly to defer to his views, and to acquiesce fully in his responses and explanations. He spoke readily, not always with grammatical accuracy, but with no appearance of hesitation or reserve, and with no apparent desire to conceal anything, nor did he repel any of my questions as impertinent. He was very plainly dressed in thin summer clothing, and with no air of sanctimony or fanaticism. In appearance, he is a portly, frank, goodnatured, rather thick-set man of fifty-five, seeming to enjoy life, and be in no particular hurry to get to heaven. His associates are plain men, evidently born and reared to a life of labor, and looking as little like crafty hypocrites or swindlers as any body of men I ever met. The absence of cant or snuffle from their manner was marked and general, yet I think I may fairly say that their Mormonism has not impoverished them— they were generally poor men when they embraced it, and are now in very comfortable circumstances— as men averaging three or four wives apiece certainly need to be.

Frederic Hudson and several other historians believed that the first interview was published in the *New York Herald* in 1859, at the time of the celebrated John Brown Raid at Harpers Ferry. Public feeling toward Brown ran high. Among others implicated in the affair was Gerrit Smith. Had Smith secretly supported the John Brown raids? One of the reporters for the *Herald* was dispatched to the well-known Quaker's residence at Peterborough, where he had a long interview with the distinguished philanthropist. This was published in full and in conversational style, but it was several months after the Greeley interview. It was written in the technique that has since become a newspaper convention.

By 1860 more reporters were writing interviews. On the eve of the Civil War several leading Rebels were interviewed at their homes. One such session was that between Alexander H. Stephens and Robert Toombs and a special correspondent for the *New York Herald.* Frederic Hudson, in his book, *Journalism in the United States from 1690 to 1872,* points out that reporters interviewed leading statesmen, army and navy officers, and politicians. These leaders realized the power of the interview in getting their facts and opinions to the readers.

Joseph B. McCullagh, Washington correspondent for the *Cincinnati Commercial,* did much to popularize the newspaper interview during the Reconstruction Period, it is noted by J. F. Essary in *Covering Washington.* He cites the case of McCullagh obtaining an interview with Alexander H. Stephens, who revealed to the reporter in a "direct quote" much of the "inside story" of the Confederacy.

More notable still were McCullagh's interviews with President Andrew Johnson. The President and the correspondent were on intimate terms, and McCullagh persuaded the executive to use the columns of the newspapers to spread his views before the public. During the Johnson impeachment proceedings, the President frequently sent for McCullagh and authorized the publication of statement after statement. He said at the time, "Everybody seems to read the interviews and nobody seems to read my messages," Essary reports.

President Johnson was criticized for speaking directly to the public through the newspapers. Yet the interview as a news-presenting device grew rapidly. General U. S. Grant, who succeeded Johnson in the presidency, often submitted to interview. R. D. B. Keim of the *New York Herald* Bureau, had ready access to General Grant, and, finding a quick market for everything the President would permit him to say, made a small fortune during the eight years of the Grant regime, Essary reveals.

Reporters in other nations followed the practice of American newsmen in writing interviews. Thus Napoleon, Antonelli, the Catholic Cardinal Bishop of London, Count Membrea, the Premier of Italy, the Prime Minister of Egypt, the Chancellor of Austria, the Emperor of Brazil, and others were interviewed.

Not all editors favored the new form of writing. *The London Daily News* in 1869 remarked, "A portion of the daily newspapers in New York are bringing the profession of journalism into contempt, so far as they can, by a kind of toadyism or flunkeyism which they call 'interviewing'!"

James Russell Lowell disliked the interview. He wrote, "Let the seventeenth century, at least, be kept sacred from the insupportable foot of the interviewer." And the *New York Nation* of 1869 characterized the interview as "generally the joint product of some humbug of a hack politician and another humbug of a newspaper reporter."

Editor's opinions concerning the new form of reporting often changed. In his booklet, "Major Interviewing, Its Principles and Functions," Edward Price Bell, of the *Chicago Daily News,* cites the reactions of the editor of the *Pall Mall Gazette.* At first the editor found the type of writing interesting and noted that the interview represented a division of labor, "the interviewee supplying the matter, the interviewer the form," which was an accurate observation. But the editor's opinion changed sharply in two years. "This American interview," he wrote in 1886, "is degrading to the interviewer, disgusting to the interviewee, and tiresome to the public."

Correspondents stationed in remote spots adopted the new form of writing. Meeting the Emperor of Brazil in Cairo in November, 1871, a correspondent for the *New York Herald* had the following conversation with him:

> Correspondent: "I see a copy of Galignani, containing an interview with Mr. Seward, from the *New York Herald,* on your table. Has your majesty read it?"
>
> Don Pedro: "I did, with interest. Mr. Seward has been a great traveler, and seems to have thoroughly improved his opportunities for observation. I shall not be able to go as far as he has done. By the way, I suppose I am now being 'interviewed,' which I believe is the term."
>
> Correspondent: "Yes, your majesty; but I will with pleasure submit my manuscript to your secretary if there should be anything you may wish expunged."
>
> Don Pedro: "Thank you; but perhaps it will not matter. I have been in a constant state of 'interview' all of my life, and consequently say nothing I am not willing to have made public. It is rather novel, though, to find a correspondent of the *New York Herald* under the shadow of the pyramids."
>
> Correspondent: "Yes, they are very enterprising men, the *Herald* correspondents, and go everywhere."

Newspaper readers had never been brought so near to the views of statesmen, merchant princes, members of royalty and politicians. The public registered great surprise on one occasion when Louis Napoleon talked with a correspondent one day at Wilhelmshöhe, and by means of cable the interview appeared in the *New York Herald* the next morning, so that Napoleon's views were known to the civilized world in forty-eight hours.

Most metropolitan newspapers speedily adopted the idea. Any person of note or anyone who had been guilty of any crime or extraordinary act was immediately called upon by a reporter. Newsmen visited state prisons for "notorious subjects." Interviewing was the mode of the day. Frederic Hudson said it became "a journalistic mania."

Ship news reporting started in New York City. Reporters met incoming vessels in search of quotes from notables. Occasionally, the newsmen faced some persons who had nothing to say. Robert Wilder, in his book, *Out of Blue*, says that between passengers and reporters there existed a guarded cordiality which resulted in a bit of give and take. He tells of Toscanini, who was forever scuttling away or thwacking a cameraman over the back with his cane. Mme Toscanini explained this delirious behavior once by saying, "He wouldn't talk to God." As far as anyone knew, he had never requested an interview.

Henry W. Grady, long before he served as editor of the *Atlanta Constitution,* worked in 1877 to 1881 as a roving correspondent for seven metropolitan newspapers. His favorite form of reporting was the interview. He called it "the neatest and handiest thing in journalism." In an article, "On Interviewing," he wrote that "Socrates, a thoroughly respectable person, introduced the custom on the streets of Athens." During these busy years Grady interviewed about five hundred prominent persons, North and South, and their friendships were invaluable to him throughout his career. Grady believed that the birth of the interview was an accident, due to the haste with which a *New York Herald* reporter wrote out a conversation with one of the participants, in the raid at Harpers Ferry in 1859.

This story may have other chapters. One of these days some graduate student in journalism may be digging through a stack of faded newspapers and find a published American interview earlier than Greeley's. But until that happens, credit for the modern interview must go to "Uncle Horace," regarded by many as the greatest editor America has ever known.

Selected List of Readings

Books

Adler, Alfred. *Understanding Human Nature.* Cleveland, World Publishing Company, 1927.

Albig, William. *Public Opinion.* New York, McGraw-Hill Book Company, 1939.

Allport, Gordon. *Personality, A Psychological Interpretation.* New York, Henry Holt and Company, 1937.

Beardsley, Monroe C. *Thinking Straight.* New York, Prentice-Hall, Inc., 1950.

Bell, Bernard Iddings. *Crowd Culture.* New York, Harper and Brothers, 1952.

Benedict, Ruth. *Patterns of Culture.* Boston, Houghton Mifflin Company, 1934.

Berger, Meyer. *The Eight Million.* New York, Simon and Schuster, 1942.

Bingham, Walter Van Dyke, and Bruce Victor Moore. *How to Interview.* New York, Harper and Brothers, 1931.

Bisch, Louis E. *Clinical Psychology.* Baltimore, Williams and Wilkins Company, 1925.

Brayfield, Arthur H. *Readings in Modern Methods of Counseling.* New York, Appleton-Century-Crofts, Inc., 1950.

Bush, Chilton R. *Newspaper Reporting of Public Affairs.* New York, Appleton-Century-Crofts, Inc., 1950.

Campbell, Walter S. *Writing Non-Fiction.* Boston, The Writer, Inc., 1944.

Casey, Robert J. *Such Interesting People.* Indianapolis, The Bobbs-Merrill Company, 1943.

Chase, Stuart. *The Proper Study of Mankind.* New York, Harper and Brothers, 1948.

Clayton, Charles C. *Newspaper Reporting Today.* New York, The Odyssey Press, Inc., 1947.

Cooley, Charles H. *Human Nature and the Social Order.* New York, Charles Scribner's Sons, 1925.

Darley, John. *The Interview in Counseling, Retraining and Re-employment Administration.* Washington, U. S. Department of Labor, 1946.

Dashiell, J. F. *Fundamentals of General Psychology.* Boston, Houghton Mifflin Company, 1937.

Drewry, John. *More Post Biographies.* Athens, University of Georgia Press, 1947.

Droke, Maxwell. *People: How to Get Them to Do What You Want Them to Do.* Indianapolis, Maxwell Droke, 1939.

Edwards, Violet (ed.). *Group Leader's Guide to Propaganda Analysis.* New York, Institute for Propaganda Analysis, Inc., 1938.

Eisenberg, Philip. *Why We Act as We Do.* New York, Alfred A. Knopf, 1947.

Erickson, Clifford E. *The Counseling Interview.* New York, Prentice-Hall, Inc., 1950.

Essary, J. F. *Covering Washington.* Boston, Houghton Mifflin Company, 1927.

Fenlason, Anne F. *Essentials in Interviewing.* New York, Harper and Brothers, 1952.

Fink, David Harold. *Be Your Real Self.* New York, Simon and Schuster, 1950.

Flesch, Rudolf. *The Art of Plain Talk*. New York, Harper and Brothers, 1946.

Flugel, J. C. *Men and Their Motives*. New York, International University Press, 1947.

Garrett, Annette. *Interviewing, Its Principles and Methods*. New York, Family Service Association of America, 1942.

Goodenough, Florence L. *Developmental Psychology*. New York, Appleton-Century-Crofts, Inc., 1945. 2nd ed.

Gorer, Geoffrey. *The American People*. New York, W. W. Norton and Company, 1948.

Gunning, Robert. *The Technique of Clear Writing*. New York, McGraw-Hill Book Company, 1952.

Hartwell, Dickson, and Andrew A. Rooney (eds.). *Off the Record*. Garden City, Doubleday and Company, 1952.

Hattwich, Melvin S. *How to Use Psychology for Better Advertising*. New York, Prentice-Hall, Inc., 1950.

Hazen, David W. *Interviewing Sinners and Saints*. Portland, Ore., Binsfords and Mort, 1942.

Healy, William. *Personality in Formation and Action*. New York, W. W. Norton and Company, 1938.

Hopper, Hedda. *From under My Hat*. Garden City, Doubleday and Company, 1952.

Hudson, Frederic. *Journalism in the United States, from 1690 to 1872*. New York, Harper and Brothers, 1937.

Hyde, Grant Milnor. *Newspaper Reporting*. New York, Prentice-Hall, Inc., 1952.

Inbau, Fred E. *Lie Detection and Criminal Investigation*. Baltimore, Williams and Wilkins Company, 1942.

Ingram, K. C. *Winning Your Way with People*. New York, Whittlesey House, 1949.

Jones, John Paul. *Modern Reporter's Handbook*. New York, Rinehart and Company, 1949.

Kardiner, Abram. *The Individual and His Society*. New York, Columbia University Press, 1939.

Kidd, W. R. *Police Interrogation.* New York, The Police Journal, 1940.

Kohler, W. *Dynamics in Psychology.* New York, Liveright Publishing Corporation, 1940.

Laird, Donald A. and Eleanor. *Sizing Up People.* New York, McGraw-Hill Book Company, 1951.

Lee, Irving J. *How to Talk with People.* New York, Harper and Brothers, 1952.

Lindeman, Eduard C. *Social Discovery.* New York, New Republic, Inc., 1924.

Lucas, Jim. *Combat Correspondent.* New York, Reynal and Hitchcock, 1944.

MacDougall, Curtis. *Interpretative Reporting.* New York, The Macmillan Company, 1950.

————. *Newsroom Problems and Policies.* New York, The Macmillan Company, 1941.

————. *Understanding Public Opinion.* New York, The Macmillan Company, 1952.

MacNeil, Neil. *Without Fear or Favor.* New York, Harcourt, Brace and Company, 1940.

————. *How to Be a Newspaperman.* New York, Harper and Brothers, 1942.

Marcosson, Isaac F. *Adventures in Interviewing.* New York, Dodd, Mead and Company, 1923.

Mead, Margaret. *Male and Female.* New York, William Morrow and Company, 1949.

Meerloo, Joost A. M. *Conversation and Communication.* New York, International University Press, 1952.

Menefee, Selden. *Assignment: U. S. A.* New York, Reynal and Hitchcock, Inc., 1943.

Miller, Webb. *I Found No Peace.* New York, Simon and Schuster, 1936.

Montagu, Ashley. *On Being Intelligent.* New York, Henry Schuman, 1951.

Moore, Robert E. *The Human Side of Selling.* New York, Harper and Brothers, 1951.

Morehouse, Ward. *Just the Other Day.* New York, McGraw-Hill Book Company, 1953.

Mott, Frank Luther (ed.). *Headlining America.* Boston, Houghton Mifflin Company, 1937 edition.

Murphy, Gardner, and Friedrich Jensen. *Approaches to Personality.* New York, Coward-McCann, Inc., 1935.

Murray, H. A. *Explorations in Personality.* New York, Oxford University Press, 1938.

Neal, Robert M. *News Gathering and News Writing.* New York, Prentice-Hall, Inc., 1940.

Neely, Twila E. *A Study of the Error in the Interview.* New York, Columbia University Press, 1937.

New York Times. Staff. *The Newspaper, Its Making and Its Meaning.* New York, Charles Scribner's Sons, 1945.

Nieman Fellows. *Newsmen's Holiday.* Cambridge, University Press, 1942.

Oestreicher, J. C. *The World Is Their Beat.* New York, Duell, Sloan and Pearce, 1945.

Oldfield, Richard C. *Psychology of the Interview.* London, Methuen and Company, Ltd., 1941.

Othman, Frederick. *Man on the Half Shell.* New York, Whittlesey House, 1947.

Overstreet, H. A. *The Great Enterprise.* New York, W. W. Norton and Company, 1952.

Overton, Grant. *Cargoes for Crusoes.* New York, D. Appleton and Company, 1924.

Patterson, Helen M. *Writing and Selling Feature Articles.* New York, Prentice-Hall, Inc., 1949.

Payne, Stanley. *The Art of Asking Questions.* Princeton, Princeton University Press, 1951.

Peale, Norman Vincent. *A Guide to Confident Living.* New York, Prentice-Hall, Inc., 1948.

Prochnow, Herbert V. *1001 Ways to Improve Your Conversation and Speeches.* New York, Harper and Brothers, 1952.

Rasmussen, Knud. *Across Arctic America.* New York, G. P. Putnam's Sons, 1927.

Reik, Theodore. *Listening with the Third Ear.* New York, Farrar, Straus and Company, 1949.

Richmond, Mary E. *Social Diagnosis.* New York, Russell Sage Foundation, 1917.

Rogers, Carl R. *Counseling and Psychotherapy.* Boston, Houghton Mifflin, 1942.

———, and John L. Wallen. *Counseling with Returned Service Men.* New York, McGraw-Hill Book Company, 1946.

Shaffer, L. E. *Psychology of Adjustment.* Boston, Houghton Mifflin Company, 1936.

Siebert, Frederick. *The Rights and Privileges of the Press.* New York, D. Appleton Century Company, 1934.

Snyder, Louis L., and Richard B. Morris (eds.). *A Treasury of Great Reporting.* New York, Simon and Schuster, 1949.

Snygg, Donald, and Arthur W. Combs. *Individual Behavior.* New York, Harper and Brothers, 1949.

Stewart, Kenneth, and John Tebbel. *Makers of Modern Journalism.* New York, Prentice-Hall, Inc., 1952.

Symonds, Percival. *The Dynamics of Human Behavior.* New York, Appleton-Century-Crofts, Inc., 1946.

———. *The Dynamics of Human Adjustment.* Appleton-Century-Crofts, Inc., 1946.

Taylor, Robert Lewis. *Doctor, Lawyer, Merchant, Chief.* Garden City, Doubleday and Company, 1948.

Walker, Stanley. *City Editor.* New York, Frederick A. Stokes Company, 1934.

Warren, Carl N. *Modern News Reporting.* New York, Harper and Brothers, 1934.

Webb, Ewing T., and John B. Morgan. *Strategy in Handling People.* Garden City, Garden City Publishing Company, 1930.

Weinland, James D., and Margaret V. Gross. *Personnel Interviewing*. New York, The Ronald Press, 1952.

Wellman, Francis L. *The Art of Cross-Examination*. New York, The Macmillan Company, 1932.

Wheeler, Elmer. *Tested Sentences That Sell*. New York, Prentice-Hall, Inc., 1938.

———. *How to Sell Yourself to Others*. New York, Prentice-Hall, Inc., 1947.

Wiggam, Albert E. *Exploring Your Mind*. Indianapolis, The Bobbs-Merrill Company, 1928.

Wilder, Robert. *Out of the Blue*. New York, G. P. Putnam's Sons, 1943.

Wilson, Earl. *Pikes Peak or Bust*. Garden City, Doubleday and Company, 1946.

Winkler, John K. *W. R. Hearst*. New York, Simon and Schuster, 1928.

Young, Pauline V. *Interviewing in Social Work*. New York, McGraw-Hill Book Company, 1935.

Zeisel, Hans. *Say It with Figures*. New York, Harper and Brothers, 1947.

Articles

Andrews, L. G. "Some Everyday Problems in Interviewing," *Industrial Management*, July, 1925.

Aston, Frank. "Triple Role Man; Carl Victor Little Deals in Satire, Books, Policy," *Scripps-Howard News*, December, 1952.

Anonymous. "A Semantic Jungle," *Time*, September 8, 1952, pp. 86–87.

———. "Art of Being Interviewed," *Scientific American*, September 7, 1918.

———. "Outline of the Interviewing Art," *Editor and Publisher*, July 21, 1932.

———. "The News Interview," *Writer's Digest*, Vol. XII, No. 1 (December, 1931).

———. "Why So Few of Us Can Ask a Question," *Current Opinion*, March, 1921.

———. "Working Press Wants to Quiz Surgeons," *Editor and Publisher*, Vol. LXXXVI, No. 1 (January 3, 1953).

Barron, Mark W. "When the Ships Come In," *The Quill*, Vol. XXII, No. 1 (January, 1935).

Bartlett, John T. "Interviewing Problems; How to Solve them," *Author and Journalist*, Vol. XXI, No. 3 (March, 1936).

Bell, Edward Price. "Major Interviewing, Its Principles and Functions," *Chicago Daily News*, Reprint No. 26, 1927.

Bevis, Joseph C. "Interviewing With Tape Recorders," *Public Opinion Quarterly*, Vol. XII, No. 2 (Summer, 1948).

Bloom, Rose L. "Practice Makes Perfect in Cultivating the Art of Interviewing," *Quill and Scroll*, Vol. X, No. 2 (December–January, 1935–36).

Brook, Thomas. "Interviews You Can Write," *Writer's Digest*, Vol. XXL, No. 10 (September, 1941).

Brown, Robert U., and George A. Brandenberg. "Reporters at Convention Ask TV 'Ground Rules,'" *Editor and Publisher*, Vol. LXXXV, No. 29 (July 12, 1952).

Cantril, Hadley. "Don't Blame It on 'Human Nature,'" *New York Times Magazine*, July 6, 1947.

Cleeton, Glen V. "What You Can't Tell about People from Their Faces," *American Magazine*, Vol. CI, No. 3 (March, 1926).

Cline, Yandell C. "Reporters Questions Often Suggest 'No' Answer When They Want 'Yes,'" *Editor and Publisher*, Vol. LX, No. 4 (June 18, 1927).

Cohen, Octavus Roy. "The Hard-Boiled Reporter and the Miracle," *Reader's Digest*, Vol. XLIX, No. 294 (October, 1946).

Conrad, Barnaby. "Don't Rely on Memory," *Author & Journalist*, Vol. XXXVII, No. 6 (June, 1952).

Cormack, B. "I Was An Interviewer," *New Republic*, April 22, 1928.

Crespi, Leo P. "The Interview Effect in Polling," *Public Opinion Quarterly*, Vol. XII, No. 1 (Spring, 1948).

Crowder, F. "Gentle Art of Questioning; Question, Most Versatile of Conversational Tools," *The Rotarian*, June, 1939.

Cummings, P. "May We Quote You on That?" *Readers Digest*, January, 1939.

DeVine, Janice. "Creating and Selling the Interview," *Writer's Year Book*, May, 1948, *Writer's Digest*.

Dickson, Frank A., Jr. "How to Interview," *Writer's Digest*, Vol. XVI, No. 8 (July, 1936), 29–31.

Dickson, John T., Harry Levinson, Arthur T. Leader, and Isabel Stamm. "Contribution to Interviewing Skills of Psychiatrists," *Journal of Social Case Work*, October, 1949.

Dollard, John. "Under What Conditions Do Opinions Predict Behavior?" *Public Opinion Quarterly*, Winter, 1948.

Downer, Bob. "Make Him Say 'Yes,' " *Writer's Digest*, August, 1949.

DuBois, Cornelius. "The Card-Sorting or Psychophysical Interview," *Public Opinion Quarterly*, Vol. XIII, No. 4 (Winter, 1949–50).

Essary, J. F. "President, Congress, and the Press Correspondents," *American Political Science Review*, Vol. XXII, No. 4 (November, 1928).

Fleming, Robert H. "Meyer Berger—Reporter," *Nieman Reports*, Vol. IV, No. 3 (July, 1950), 11–14.

Frank, Gerold. "Writing the Personality Sketch," *Writer's Digest*, August, 1939.

Frank, Stanley, and Paul Sann. "Paper Dolls," *Saturday Evening Post*, May 20, 1944.

Friedman, Ralph. "There's No One Way to Interview," *Au-*

thor & Journalist, Vol. XXXVIII, No. 2 (February, 1953).

Gale, P. "Psychology of the Interview," *The Writer,* October, 1943.

Garrod, Pat. "Let Them Talk," *The Writer,* Vol. X, No. 4 (October, 1952).

Graham, Sheilah. "Adventures of an Interviewer," *Delineator,* Vol. CXXVII, No. 5 (November, 1935).

Greene, C. M. "Advice to Young Interviewers," *Bookman,* Vol. L, No. 5 (January, 1920).

Gruenther, Homer H. "MacDonald Picks Own Assignments," *Editor and Publisher,* Vol. LXIII, No. 33 (January 3, 1931).

Hainline, Joe. "Televised Interview Is Seen as the Public's Gain," *The Quill,* Vol. XL, No. 10 (October, 1952).

Hamilton, Jack. "What's Your Angle? How to do a Biographical Article," *Writer's Digest,* Vol. XXVIII, No. 3 (February, 1948).

Heard, A. "Interviewing Southern Politicians," *American Political Science Review,* December, 1950.

Henry, Marguerite. "Adventures of a Ghost Writer," *Writer's Digest,* Vol. XV, No. 11 (October, 1935), 37.

Hills, Lee. "Creative Newspapering Demands Imagination to Ask Extra Questions," *The Quill,* Vol. XXXIX, No. 8 (August, 1951).

Hinckley, Robert, and Anne F. Fenlason. "Mental Hygiene Interviewing: A Therapeutic Approach," *American Journal of Orthopsychiatry,* April, 1942.

Hovland, Carl I., and Walter Weiss. "The Influence of Source Credibility on Communication Effectiveness," *Public Opinion Quarterly,* Vol. XV, No. 4 (Winter, 1951–52).

Hubbard, Alfred W. "Phrasing Questions," *Journal of Marketing,* July, 1950.

Hunt, Morton M. "Soft-Boiled Subjects Talk," *Writer's Digest,* Vol. XXXII, No. 4 (March, 1952).

Lazarfeld, Paul F. "The Art of Asking Why," *National Marketing Review*, Vol. I, (1935).

———. "The Controversy Over Detailed Interviews—An Offer for Negotiation," *Public Opinion Quarterly*, Vol. VII, No. 1 (Spring, 1944).

Lindstrom, Carl. "The Writing Isn't Good Enough," *Nieman Reports*, Vol. VI, No. 1 (January, 1952).

Linton, Ralph. "The Personality of Peoples," *Scientific American*, August, 1949.

Little, Arthur. "Getting the Material," *The Quill*, Vol. XX, No. 2 (February, 1932).

Lyons, Louis M. "Can Your Readers Keep Up With the News?" *Nieman Reports*, Vol. VII, No. 3 (July, 1952).

Mann, Dorothea. "Authors and the Interviewer," *Bookman*, Vol. LXIX, No. 5 (July, 1929).

Martson, D. R. "Pointers on Interviewing," *The Writer*, October, 1943.

McDowell, Charles, Jr. "Lo, The Feature Writer! A Cure for His Woes," *Editor and Publisher*, Vol. LXXXV, No. 33 (August 9, 1952).

Merton, R. K., and P. L. Kindall. "Focused Interview," *American Journal of Sociology*, May, 1946.

Morgan, Roy. "A Note on Question Wording," *Public Opinion Quarterly*, Vol. XII, No. 2 (Summer, 1948).

Nixon, Raymond B. "Henry W. Grady, Reporter," *Journalism Quarterly*, Vol. XII, No. 4 (December, 1935), 341–56.

Ogdon, William. "Getting Them to Talk," *The Quill*, Vol. XXII, No. 2 (February, 1934)

Painton, Frederick C. "The Hoosier Letter-Writer," *Saturday Evening Post*, October 2, 1943.

Payne, Stanley L. "Case Study in Questions Complexity," *Public Opinion Quarterly*, Vol. XIII, No. 4 (Winter, 1949–50).

Pollard, James E. "The White House News Conference as a

Channel of Communication," *Public Opinion Quarterly,* Vol. XV, No. 4 (Winter, 1951–52).

Pryor, Hubert. "Bigwigs Under Fire," *Look,* Vol. XVII, No. 3 (February 10, 1953).

Rice, S. A. "Contagious Bias in the Interview; A Methodological Note," *American Journal of Sociology,* November, 1929.

Ridder, Walter T. "The Decline and Fall of the Press Conference," *The Quill,* Vol. XL, No. 9 (September, 1952), 7–14.

Robinson, Henry Morton. "What I Know About You!" *The Rotarian,* January, 1937, pp. 20–23.

Roethlisberger, F. J. "Barriers to Communication Between Men," *Communications in Today's World, Bulletin* of Northwestern University, Vol. XX, No. 25 (April 21, 1952).

Ross, Betty. "Isaac Marcosson Says," *Writer's Monthly,* Vol. XXV, No. 3 (February, 1925).

Rugg, Donald. "Experiments in Wording Questions: II," *Public Opinion Quarterly,* Vol. V, No. 4 (March, 1941).

———, and Hadley Cantril. "Wording of Questions in Public Opinion Polls," *Journal of Abnormal and Social Psychology,* October, 1942.

Sheatsley, Paul B. "Some Uses of Interviewer-Report Forms," *Public Opinion Quarterly,* Vol. XI, No. 4 (Winter, 1947–48).

Smith, Harry L., and Herbert Hyman. "The Biasing Effect of Interviewer Expectations on Survey Results," *Public Opinion Quarterly,* Vol. XIV, No. 3 (Fall, 1950).

Sonenfield, Peg. "Home Sweet Folks at Home," *Scripps-Howard News,* Vol. V, No. 3 (December, 1950), 14.

Sontheimer, Morton. "Inside an Article," *Writer's Digest,* March, 1951.

Sprague, J. R. "Interviewing Business Men," *Saturday Evening Post*, Vol. CCVI, No. 31 (January 27, 1934), 23–24.

Stapel, Jan. "The Convivial Respondent," *Public Opinion Quarterly*, Vol. XI, No. 4 (Winter, 1947–48).

Strickland, Eunice Jones. "Let Them Talk," *Writer's Digest*, September, 1946.

Strakosch, Avery. "The Ghost Talks," *Writer's Digest*, April, 1939.

Terris, Fay. "Are Poll Questions Too Difficult?" *Public Opinion Quarterly*, Vol. XIII, No. 2 (Summer, 1949).

Turnbull, George. "Some Notes on the History of the Interview," *Journalism Quarterly*, Vol. XIII, No. 3 (September, 1935).

Ueland, Berenda. "How to Write an Autobiography," *Writer's Digest*, September, 1941.

Walker, Stanley. "What Makes a Good Reporter?" *American Mercury*, February, 1946.

Watts, M. S. "Chats With Lions; an Interviewer Is a Big Game Hunter," *Scholastic*, February 17, 1947.

Weisinger, Mort. "The Million Dollar Article," *Writer's Digest*, November, 1949.

Wetstein, A. "Practical Formulaes for Interviews," *Saturday Evening Post*, October 14, 1933.

Wicklein, J. F. "Say Something for the Press," *The Rotarian*, October, 1951.

Wiggam, Albert Edward. "Sizing Up the Other Fellow," *American Magazine*, Vol. CX, No. 1 (July, 1930), 40–41.

Williams, Douglas. "Basic Instructions for Interviewers," *The Public Opinion Quarterly*, Vol. VI, No. 4 (Winter, 1942), 635–41.

Williamson, Kennedy. "The Interview Article," *The Writer*, June, 1935.

Wolfson, V. M. "Inside View of the Interview," *The Writer*, January, 1951.

Ziff, William B. "Your Gestures Give You Away," *Your Life,* August, 1951.

Zolotow, Maurice. "The New Way to Study a Subject," *Writer's Digest,* September, 1951.

Index

217

UNIVERSITY OF OKLAHOMA PRESS

NORMAN